Opportunity abounds. Are you ready?

The housing market is full of potential: historically low interest rates, attractively priced housing stock and millions of prospective buyers who still believe in the value of homeownership. Right now, the Millennial generation (those born between 1979 and 2000) represents *the biggest first-time homebuyer business opportunity in the history of our country!*[1]

Sure, there's a lot of negativity out there. But there's also plenty of opportunity. And the fact is, someone is going to be successful at tapping it. Is that someone you? Are you doing everything you can to capture every prospective sale this market offers?

**SPEAKING OF OPPORTUNITY...
Did you know there are 6 million more Millennials in the prime first-time homebuyer age range than there were Baby Boomers?**[1]

Today, more than ever, buyers and sellers rely on us for professional service and moral support. If we want to win their business and future referrals, we must be at the top of our game. To help you stay there, we're pleased to bring you this special edition of Brian Buffini and Joe Niego's newest book. Leverage the content to help you capitalize on the potential that exists.

As the nation's leading retail mortgage lender, Wells Fargo Home Mortgage remains committed to relationships—with our customers and real estate industry colleagues—that last far beyond closing d~   And we're here for you in all the ways that count, with our proprie~   ~oachPriority®️ tools, programs and support to help you b~'   ~ove buyers and close deals.

Brad Blackwell
Executive Vice President
National Retail Sales Manager

~dz

~ive Vice President
~ational Retail Sales Manager

1. Source: U.S. Census Data

EQUAL HOUSING
LENDER

ENDORSEM

If you own or are thinking of starting a business, this book is more important than a computer. Brian and Joe's thoughts and ideas have helped our own small business survive and thrive.

— LOU HOLTZ, former head coach, University of Notre Dame;
inducted into the College Football Hall of Fame

....

When Brian Buffini speaks and writes, I take out my notepad! His big ideas have had a big impact on hundreds of thousands of entrepreneurs and small business owners. I encourage you to read this book and start growing today!

— JON GORDON, best-selling author of "The Energy Bus" and "Soup"

....

As long-time champions of the entrepreneurial spirit, my dad Zig and I give high praise to Brian Buffini and Joe Niego's "Takin' Care of Business: The BIG IDEA for Small Business." In this follow-up to "Work By Referral. Live the Good Life!," you'll find out how to leverage your time, energy and money for maximum impact and profitability. Don't miss it!

— TOM ZIGLAR, son of Zig Ziglar; CEO, Ziglar, Inc.

....

A must read for every business owner and entrepreneur! "Takin' Care of Business: The BIG IDEA for Small Business" is the ultimate key to leveraging your time, energy, and money to secure an ever-increasing amount of sales and a lucrative financial future. Brian Buffini and Joe Niego combine expert wisdom, practical strategies, and real-world anecdotes that will empower you to achieve breakthrough success!

— IVAN MISNER, NY Times best-selling author;
founder of BNI® and Referral Institute®

....

There is no more revered leader, coach and trainer in our business than Brian Buffini. Now in his new book, "Takin' Care of Business," he shares a lifetime of learning about how leaders of small businesses can really turn up their performance and create enduring organizations that are fun, fulfilling and profitable. As we turn the corner on our industry, there is no better time for leaders, whether in sales or sales management, to grasp the fundamentals outlined in this valuable new book.

— STEVE MURRAY, editor, REAL Trends, Inc.;
owner of REAL Trends Consulting, Inc.

ENTS

"Takin' Care of Business: The BIG IDEA for Small Business" is THE essential guide for everyone from new business owners to seasoned business pros. In their follow-up to "Work By Referral. Live the Good Life!," Brian Buffini and Joe Niego do it again, providing entrepreneurs with critical tactics and strategies for building a wildly successful business and significant life.

— TONY SCHWARTZ, CEO, The Energy Project;
author of "Be Excellent at Anything" and "The Power of Full Engagement"

....

This book is amazing! The economic challenges facing today's business men and women are the greatest in our history. This book is a refreshing look at how to take on those challenges and win!

— DAVE LINIGER, chairman/cofounder, RE/MAX, LLC

....

The straightforward prose at work in "Takin' Care of Business" cleverly disguises a sophisticated strategic framework for workplace success. Enthusiastic entrepreneurs and professional managers alike will find the read a worthy investment of precious time.

— PHIL SOPER, president/CEO, Brookfield Real Estate Services/Royal LePage

....

Those lucky enough to pick up Brian Buffini and Joe Niego's new book, "Takin' Care of Business: The BIG IDEA for Small Business," are in for more than a great read... they will also walk away with a clear and enlightened view of what it takes to make a business successful. This book is filled with profound and useful information, allowing business owners to transform their businesses if they put into place the very ideas and tips that Brian and Joe share with readers. I highly recommend this book to those who want to excel and propel their businesses to a much higher level.

— KIM MARIE BRANCH-PETTID, CEO, LeTip International

....

"Takin' Care of Business" is a must-read for all entrepreneurs, whether you are breaking out on your own for the first time or you are a veteran business owner. If you internalize the principles in this book, you will make your business a permanent success. A fabulous read!

— HYRUM SMITH, cofounder of Franklin/Covey; CEO, Gallileo Initiative

"Takin' Care of Business" is brilliant in its simple approach to success. Most business owners and entrepreneurs know the basics but clutter their success path with "gobbledegook." "Takin' Care of Business" has filtered through that. This book will be a success manual for years to come for businesses big and small. I know it has re-focused me, and for that I am grateful. Brian and Joe have a winner on their hands. Congratulations on the clarity this book delivers to its reader.

– WALTER SCHNEIDER, cofounder of RE/MAX Ontario-Atlantic Canada, Inc.

....

"Takin' Care of Business: The BIG IDEA for Small Business" builds on the proven referral-marketing systems Brian Buffini and Joe Niego pioneered to help thousands of real estate professionals across the country. If you're looking to create a rock-solid business and a rich financial legacy, this book is for you!

– WES FOSTER, chairman/CEO, Long & Foster Companies

....

Brian and Joe's book is an essential read for the success of your small business. The examples he uses will allow you to see where you are being willfully blind within your own company, and will give you the processes to cause the results you want to see.

– LOU TICE, author of "Smart Talk"; cofounder of The Pacific Institute

....

Brian Buffini and Joe Niego are geniuses at helping people achieve both success and significance in business and in life. Read this book and apply it in all you do. The results will be amazing.

– DR. NIDO R. QUBEIN, president, High Point University; chairman, Great Harvest Bread Co.

From the authors of "Work by Referral. Live the Good Life!"

BRIAN BUFFINI & JOE NIEGO

Takin' Care of
BUSINESS

THE BIG IDEA
FOR SMALL BUSINESS

Published by Buffini & Company, Inc.
Carlsbad, California, U.S.A.

ISBN: 978-0-9820260-1-4

Printed in the United States of America

DEDICATION

To every courageous person who ever had the gumption
to own his or her own business, we honor the belief you have
in yourself, the confidence you have in your abilities
and the faith you have in your future.

You are the fabric of every great society.

It would bring us great joy if this book in some way
helps you achieve a greater level of success.

Thanks to Bachman Turner Overdrive who came out with the theme song
for all small-business owners: "Takin' Care of Business."

ACKNOWLEDGEMENTS

It has been said, *"Tough times don't build character. They reveal it."*

~ A few special thanks ~

Beverly and Julie
Thanks for your never-ending love and support. Our journey through life is so much more enjoyable because of you.

Our kids, the *A Team* and the *Fab 5*
Thanks for your unique and youthful insight and for helping us think outside the box. Our relationships with you provide a richer and fuller perspective on life.

David Lally
Thanks for always being there. Your *fingers of fury* never missed an impactful idea or a solid sound bite.

Terry Niego
Thanks for keeping us on track and tapping into your wealth of experience.

Anita Slomski
Thanks for your thorough editing. Your insightful questions always helped us remember the reader.

Terri King
Thanks for adding your *touch of class*.

The Servant Leaders at Buffini & Company
Thanks for your tireless efforts to impact and improve the lives of people. Your dedication makes a difference.

Special thanks to our clients who have allowed us to use their stories to inspire others.

TABLE OF CONTENTS

Business— The Great Adventure

Brian Buffini

In the business world, everyone is paid in two coins: cash and experience. Take the experience first; the cash will come later.

– Harold S. Geneen

Business—
The Great Adventure

Brian Buffini

On June 4, 1986, I boarded a TWA 747 at Dublin Airport bound for New York City. At the gate, I hugged my father and mother goodbye. The tears in my mother's eyes reflected the all-too-familiar understanding Irish parents have that their adult children may never return home again. For 150 years, Ireland's greatest export has been its people, and my parents knew I was about to become one more emigration statistic.

My dad, a house painter, wanted me to have better opportunities in life than he had. But without the right connections, ZIP code or schooling, my prospects were greatly limited in Ireland. My dad knew that humble beginnings were no barrier to success in the States.

When I got off the plane at my final destination in San Diego, California, I was carrying $92 in my wallet and a duffle bag containing all my worldly possessions. Nineteen years old, I was filled with optimism and apprehension, excitement and absolute fear.

All these years later, the emotion and experiences of that time still create a picture in my mind as if it happened just yesterday. I've often thought, "What advice would I have for that young lad today?" This book would be a summary of that advice. That young man had no idea of the fortune he would build. He had no concept of what the pain of losing it all would mean, or the lessons that would be learned in re-building his fortune—not just for himself, but for his family also.

My road to success has not been a straight path, nor has it been without many trials and tribulations. But for the better part of three decades, I've had the excitement *and* struggles of owning many businesses, which have given me a great understanding of how a small business works. I was a painter and decorator. I sold T-shirts off a cart by the beach. I was a real estate agent. I owned retail stores, a gas station and a hotel. I've been both a property developer and an investor. And a partridge in a pear tree!

Today I lead an organization called Buffini & Company with more than 200 employees dedicated to helping small businesses become more successful. Based on my experience running a wide variety of businesses and in talking with thousands of small business owners in many industries, I've realized that we all share common risks, emotions, challenges, stresses, joys and dreams.

I've had times of incredible struggle, seasons of stagnation where I couldn't grow my business, and I've made dumb decisions that undermined the economic stability of my family. I definitely earned a master's in business from the school of hard knocks. But the highs and lows of my journey have been invaluable in teaching me what to do and what mistakes not to repeat. Here are my top 10 Wall of Shame business mistakes:

Mistake #1. I came across a man with a new product who was very engaging and insisted his product was so good it would sell itself. It didn't, but I believed him!

Mistake #2. I've launched a business without taking into account the financial cost. No budgets, no forecast, just wishful thinking and some quick math. I lost my shirt on that one.

Mistake #3. I've ignored the feedback of those I trust when they raised a red flag about a business venture.

Mistake #4. I've built overly optimistic financial models, which required everything to go right for the business to make a profit. I paid the price for my unbridled optimism.

Mistake #5. I've asked family and close friends to invest in my business venture and promised them a high return on investment. It unnecessarily strained those relationships.

Mistake #6. I've had job openings that I've filled with people I knew because it was convenient instead of finding the most qualified person for the job (and if they happened to be a friend or family member, that was an added bonus).

Mistake #7. In the past, I've focused much of my time and energy on building the business' operation and working on processes, which caused me to abdicate the vital role of Sales & Marketing to someone else.

Mistake #8. I was so intent on finding the next customer that I forgot to cultivate the relationships I already had with past customers.

Mistake #9. I created a business in an industry that I had no prior knowledge of or experience in and had little time to learn it.

Mistake #10. To round out the above list, I tried to force business growth that was too rapid—causing my company to have too little cash on hand and not handle the ebbs and flows in the market. And as a result, I wasn't always able to pay the taxman on time!

Maybe you can relate to some of these mistakes, or perhaps you are experiencing some of these challenges right now. But let me encourage you by saying that experiencing the pain of these mistakes ultimately turned on the light bulb for me. Not only did I not repeat the mistakes, I discovered the Big Idea for Small Business success, which over the years has created a recession-proof fortune for me and for my family that will provide opportunities for my children and for their kids, too. My business partner, Joe Niego, and I are delighted to be able to share the Big Idea for Small Business with you in the chapters of this book. When this one Big Idea becomes your main focus, your small business can become big.

I met Joe at a real estate conference at the St. Francis Drake Hotel in San Francisco in 1992. Joe was one of the most successful real estate agents in the United States and had a great mind for business. Within days of meeting each other, we realized we were brothers from different mothers. Not only have we become the best of friends, we've formed a perfect partnership over the years in which we brainstorm ideas, refer good books to each other and help each other through the daily challenges of being self-employed.

The truths and principles that Joe and I present in this book will, when followed, keep you from making all the mistakes I have made and help you reach a new level of success in your business.

Since the formation of Buffini & Company in 1995, Joe and I have had the chance to present our ideas and systems to more than 2 million business owners at live events and seminars, and our training systems are now taught in 37 countries. I share this not to impress you, but to impress upon you that the systems, strategies and ideas we'll share with you in this book work in hundreds of industries across many different markets, and they'll work for you, too.

It's our hope that you'll take this book to heart, apply these principles and modify your tactics. Owning a business that supports your life and helps you achieve your dreams is one of the greatest thrills you can have professionally. So read, learn and implement.

The good life awaits!

CHAPTER TWO

The Light Bulb
Goes On

Brian Buffini

*There is nothing more powerful than
an idea whose time has come.*

– Victor Hugo

The Light Bulb Goes On

Brian Buffini

Economic booms can be great for business. They can increase your income and your confidence and give your business tremendous momentum. But booms also have a downside. During a boom it's easy to drift away from the fundamentals, *especially the fundamentals of generating new customers,* because customers come looking for you when the market is hot. When a recession or economic downturn hits, this drift that takes place in most businesses becomes apparent. In both up and down markets, we have a tendency to get caught up in the current outcomes—which may not be an accurate reflection of a business' true state.

My wife and I have six kids, and they've all taken after their mom to become great athletes. My eldest son, AJ, is an outstanding football player. Like most young people who are working out or active all the time, he has the metabolism of an incinerator. After picking him up from practice one night, he asked me to stop for a *snack* on our way home.

Now I was thinking that we'd pick up some munchies at a gas station, but AJ had something else in mind. He asked to stop at an In-N-Out Burger where he proceeded to order a *4X4.* No, that's not a truck; it's a burger with four patties, four slices of cheese and all the trimmings. He also ordered the largest size of fries, a vanilla shake, and a large lemonade and devoured everything on the drive home. Then shortly after we got home, I walked into the kitchen to find AJ building a sandwich that would make Scooby Doo proud.

This was a golden opportunity for one of those father/son *chats,* and I spoke with AJ about establishing good eating habits. It was important to reinforce the fact that later in life his metabolism wouldn't work at quite the same pace. Anyone over the age of 40 knows exactly what I mean.

Well, a hot market is to business what an 18-year-old's metabolism is to the body. You can do the wrong thing and still be rewarded—*in the short term!* The good news for AJ is that he has a few years to get his eating habits turned around. The bad news for you and me is that just 18 months of bad habits and poor fundamentals can do damage to a business that can take years to repair—and in some cases prove fatal.

An economic downturn or recession is ultimately a great thing for your business—if you can survive it. It exposes any weaknesses and gaps in your fundamentals and gives you an opportunity, *if you fix those problems,* to create a business you can depend on in good times and bad.

In this chapter, you'll learn the three fundamentals every business must have in place in order to succeed in any economic environment. You'll also discover which fundamental carries five times the weight of the other two. You'll discover the Big Idea and how an adjustment in your thinking and a shift in your focus can produce a dramatic increase in your business.

Does Your Business Have a Leg to Stand On?

The image of a three-legged stool usually represents the three fundamentals of Sales & Marketing, Customer Service and Financial Management. If you put your weight on a stool and one leg is broken or two legs are missing, you're going to fall flat on your back. Or, as is the case with many small businesses, the three legs may be there, but they're not strong enough to withstand market changes, customer shifts or an economic downturn. And just when the business owner needs to be supported, they crack under pressure.

Your Business

Sales & Marketing

Financial Management

Customer Service

1. Sales & Marketing

> Definition of Marketing: promotion, advertising, networking and lead generation for your business.

> Definition of Sales: the daily focus of 1) turning potential leads into customers and 2) generating more business from existing customers.

2. Customer Service

> Definition of Customer Service: the creation, production and fulfillment of your product or service to your customer. It also includes operations, logistics and the administration of your business.

3. Financial Management

> Definition of Financial Management: overseeing the income, expenditures, profits and cash flow of your business.

When I share the three fundamentals with audiences at live events, I ask them to take a personal inventory of their business' fundamentals by grading themselves on a scale of 1 to 10 (1 being the weakest) on the strength of each leg of their stool.

Sales & Marketing

If you give yourself a **10** in Sales & Marketing, you're someone who is focused on generating a customer each day. This does not mean that you spend every hour of your workday looking for the next customer. What it does mean, however, is that you dedicate time every day for lead generation and customer acquisition.

Rate your Sales & Marketing performance from 1 to 10:

Customer Service

You're a **10** in Customer Service if your customers are so delighted they're buying you gifts and writing you notes of appreciation. You're more concerned about the customers' experience than they are, and you're committed to not only meeting expectations but exceeding them so that customers become advocates for your business. While it's difficult to be objective about the Customer Service you provide, the ultimate gauge is the percentage of your customers that promote your business. If 30 percent of your business comes from repeat business or referrals, you might give yourself a **3**; if it's 50 percent, award yourself a **5**, and so on.

Rate your Customer Service from 1 to 10:

Financial Management

You're a **10** in Financial Management if you have a working budget for your business, a monthly profit and loss statement, and at least three months' cash reserves to cover business expenses. You also have a home budget and six months' cash reserves in your personal finances.

This is a good rule of thumb for the average business employing 20 or fewer people. If you fall short of these guidelines, don't feel bad. Less than 3 percent of those who begin in our Business Coaching program exhibit solid Financial Management, yet 90 percent have all the pieces in place after just 24 months. So there is hope!

Rate your Financial Management from 1 to 10:

Sales & Marketing	Customer Service	Financial Management	Your Business
(1–10)	(1–10)	(1–10)	Total (Out of a total of 1,000)
	X	X	=

Now multiply the numbers. Most people give themselves a **5** in each of the three categories, for a score of 125 out of a possible 1,000 points. Now take your total score and multiply it by $1,000 to get your potential income. A score of 125, for example, translates into an income of $125,000.

Sales & Marketing	Customer Service	Financial Management	Your Business
(1–10)	(1–10)	(1–10)	Total (Out of a total of 1,000)
5	X 5	X 5	= 125

Anytime we do a self-assessment test, it's difficult to be objective about our own performance. This assessment will identify which area of your business plays the most significant role in your future success.

The First Big Aha!

All three legs of the stool are vital, but not all are equally weighted. A daily commitment to Sales & Marketing is the most important ingredient to small-business success, so an hour spent on Sales & Marketing is worth five hours spent on either of the other two categories. At Buffini & Company, we have coached more than 75,000 small-business owners and, without question, their biggest problem is that they have an inconsistent source of new customers. Most small businesses do not dedicate sufficient time, energy and resources to customer acquisition. Many have no systems for cultivating leads at all!

Recently my wife and I rebuilt our home after losing it to the California wildfires. This was in the midst of the economic downturn, so we were able to find the finest tradespeople at competitive prices. We'd heard so many nightmarish stories of contractors starting a job and not finishing, runaway costs and overruns, shoddy work and lack of professionalism. But our general contractor, Mo Curcic, did a spectacular job for us. The major reason: he had found an abundance of top-quality tradespeople to work on the job.

> *A daily commitment to Sales & Marketing is the most important ingredient to small-business success.*

All of the subcontractors I spoke with told me they had been busy for many years but now work was scarce. Although they were thankful to be working on our home, they had no idea where they would get their next jobs. All of these people had generated their business in the past by *word of mouth*. None of them had a system for proactively generating a lead, and now when faced with a recession, they didn't know how to go about finding customers. *The only thing these subcontractors knew to do was reduce their prices!*

To return to our exercise, multiply the score you gave yourself in Sales & Marketing by five. The new total number is a much more accurate reflection of your business' potential if you consistently generate quality leads in a systematic way. So instead of a score of 125 and an income of $125,000, focusing on Sales & Marketing will yield a score of 625—and an income of $625,000.

Sales & Marketing	Customer Service	Financial Management	Your Business
(1–10)	(1–10)	(1–10)	**Total** (Out of a total of 1,000)
25 X	**5** X	**5** =	**625**

Now don't get me wrong, Customer Service is in my DNA. I come from five generations of painter/decorators who committed to doing a terrific job for every client. We've dedicated three chapters in this book to the art of Customer Service, because without it, you'll go out of business.

But here is the Big Idea for Small Business:

CUSTOMER SERVICE IS YOUR *JOB*;
SALES & MARKETING IS YOUR *BUSINESS*.

Regardless of the language, country or culture, small-business owners make the same mistake: they become totally focused on the products or services they offer and neglect what needs to be done to grow their businesses.

Rachel's Story:
Build a Business You Can Depend On

I've met so many people over the years who are frustrated and dispirited in their businesses yet are extremely skilled at their craft. One such person was Rachel Kupin, who came to our Turning Point event in 2007 (a two-day intensive training seminar on the Working by Referral system that Joe and I teach).

A tax advisor from Carlsbad, California, Rachel joined our Business Coaching program soon after she attended the Turning Point. (Our Business Coaching program personalizes the systems taught at the Turning Point and holds people accountable for achieving specific goals. In essence, we hold peoples' feet to the fire to perform the activities they've committed to doing.) At the time she started with us, Rachel was one of those people who took every class and certification to stay abreast of trends in her industry and kept up to date with the latest software. But as dedicated as she was to her profession and improving her skills, Rachel did not have a healthy business. She had too few clients, and some clients were difficult to work with or tardy in paying their bills. Her income was far below what she had hoped for when she first entered her profession.

The light bulb came on for Rachel when she realized her business was filled with poor-quality customers because she was willing to work with anyone who called her office. These demanding clients took more of her time than good clients. They were high maintenance, not as enjoyable to serve and often less profitable. With coaching, Rachel recognized that she would have a choice of customers once she created and directed a flow of new leads into her business.

This process of changing your mindset from Customer Service to Sales & Marketing is often difficult. "I'm not a salesperson," Rachel protested, "I'm a tax advisor!" But we laid out the Working by Referral methodologies for her, boiled down into what we call the Win-the-Day Formula, which we'll outline for you in Chapter Five. We helped her develop a professional approach to marketing with a daily discipline of lead generation, and she began to embrace the process of change. Rachel transformed herself from a really good accountant to a really good businesswoman.

From a client base of 35 that she handled on her own, Rachel has grown her tax practice business to a team of three who ensure excellent service for more than 400 clients. While many of Rachel's peers' businesses failed during the recent recession, her business expanded. Rachel still faces the challenges and difficulties that all small-business owners have from time to time, but now she truly has a business on which she can depend.

In the following chapters we'll be sharing stories of people from many industries and walks of life who've applied our Working by Referral system with tremendous results. Sometimes these stories sound too good to be true, but our clients' successes speak for themselves. For example, 8,000 of our clients are in the real estate industry, and last year they earned more than six times the national average of a typical Realtor®. What we're teaching here is not a *get-rich-quick* scheme. As Thomas Edison said, "Success comes dressed in overalls and looks a lot like work." Working by Referral takes effort, but it's a small price to pay to have your business standing strong on all three legs.

SECTION I

Sales & Marketing

Takin' Care of
Marketing

Joe Niego

People don't believe what you tell them.
They rarely believe what you show them.
They often believe what their friends tell them.
They always believe what they tell themselves.

– Marketing Dictum

Takin' Care of Marketing

Joe Niego

On September 27, 1994, I walked into my real estate broker's office anticipating a routine meeting about policy. His actual agenda knocked me back on my heels. The broker said that there was a general disquiet in the company of almost 40 agents. At that time I was producing almost half the sales volume of the entire organization, but many of the other agents, who were hurting for sales, were threatening to leave the company. With fewer real estate agents, total sales for the company would drop—a situation the broker was trying desperately to avoid.

Starting immediately, my broker said, the new policy was that any leads I generated would now be distributed among all the agents in the company. All inquiries from my For Sale signs, ads or marketing would also be equally dispersed to the other agents.

I couldn't believe what I was hearing. Everything I believed about the free market and all the principles my father had taught me about hard work ultimately paying off were undermined by this new policy. My entrepreneurial passion was no longer being rewarded. The broker figured I had no choice but to accept his dictum. Of the more than 50 clients I was representing at that time, all contracts were with the brokerage. If I didn't go along with his plan, the broker could take all those transactions away from me, putting more than $200,000 in commissions at stake—a small fortune to a kid from the south side of Chicago. He had me backed into a corner. For the rest of the afternoon, I discussed the situation with my sister Terry and brother Quinn, both of whom worked for me. "This is so unfair. It's just not right," Terry kept saying through her tears. We had two options: stay and accept the new policy, or open our own enterprise that would honor an entrepreneurial vision.

Emotions and tension were running high when my phone rang. A client wanted to change our appointment time for that very evening. My brother and sister were staring at me. What was I going to say?

"Sure, we're still on for tonight. I'll see you at 7:30. I'm looking forward to putting your home on the market and getting it sold for you!"

As I hung up the phone, Terry looked at me in disbelief. "How can you even think about going on an appointment at a time like this? We have some important decisions to make about our future."

"You're right," I said. "Congratulations! We've just opened Niego Real Estate!" It was 4:10 p.m., eight hours from the time the broker upended my career at his company.

On the south side of Chicago, Niego Real Estate (*www.niegoreal estate.com*) continues to help families sell and purchase their dream homes. If you ever happen to pass by, look for the date and time etched into the glass above the door: "Open for Business – September 27th, 1994, 4:10 p.m." That was the exact moment I knew I would be successful in my own business. I didn't have the necessary office equipment yet, but what I did have was invaluable: the relationships with clients and a database I had proactively developed.

Fortunately, most people who open a small business have the opportunity to engage in more foresight and planning. There are others, however, who begin a small business under duress similar to mine. Maybe getting laid off from their jobs was the impetus they needed to pursue their passions. Some may have experienced a death in the family that forced them back into the workforce. Or maybe they just got sick and tired of the corporate world and decided to go into business for themselves.

No matter what caused you to start your own business you must focus on the Big Idea for Small Business to make it successful.

Rock 'n' Roll

In 1975, the rock everyone was talking about had nothing to do with Led Zeppelin, The Rolling Stones or Fleetwood Mac. It was an ordinary, garden-variety rock that you could find in your yard or see kids kicking down the street on their way to school. And the reason it had captured imaginations was 99 percent marketing genius. Gary Dahl, a marketing executive from Los Gatos, California, convinced people to pay $3.95 (almost 20 bucks in today's money) to buy a Pet Rock, which came packaged in its own crate and included a user's manual. In just six months, Dahl became a multimillionaire selling an object that brought no logical value to its purchaser.

Although the Pet Rock was a fad that lasted less than a year, it is a brilliant testament to the power of marketing. Granted, most small businesses don't have the advertising budgets and wherewithal to promote their products and services as Dahl did. But the point is, by generating buzz and demand for what was just a plain-old rock, Dahl brought the Pet Rock to the forefront of the country's attention. Many small businesses that offer a more enduring and useful product or service don't even make it into consumers' conversations because they engage in ineffective marketing—or none at all.

In this chapter you'll learn to make the Big Idea for Small Business—which is that Sales & Marketing is the most important aspect of your business—come alive. See how your current approach aligns with our principles. Where do you need to make changes so that your business can be *rock* solid?

Build a Better Mousetrap

Build a better mousetrap and the world will beat a path to your door. In reality, this cliché is pure myth. Many business owners make the mistake of always trying to build a better mousetrap. "If I can just get a better product, my business will take off," they'll say. Or, "I can be successful if I can just spend more time and energy improving the products I have." There is an assumption that a great product or service will sell itself, and that's simply not true. Nothing sells itself.

As a veteran small-business owner of more than 24 years, I've been the confidante of many people in my network—real estate brokers, attorneys, financial planners, insurance agents and accountants—regarding their business struggles. Most of these small companies simply don't have enough customers. I know these people to be intelligent and competent at what they do. They're excellent at Customer Service and are honest and extremely personable. So why wouldn't customers be beating paths to their doors? Because competency and good character aren't enough to make a business successful!

> *Nothing sells itself.*

My financial planner, Barry, is a prime example. I've worked with Barry for more than 20 years and I believe he is one of the best in the business. Barry's advice has allowed me to outperform the market and avoid disastrous outcomes from stock market corrections. He's smart, personable and extremely honest. In short, he's a financial whizz with a solid moral fiber. Based on his level of competency and strong character, you would think he would have more business than he was capable of handling. But that wasn't the case. Despite all his years as a financial planner, his business was stagnant. Interestingly, at the close of our financial meetings, Barry would often ask me how it was that my business grew year after year. He asked me for my

> *It's less about building a better mousetrap and more about selling and marketing the mousetrap you already have.*

productivity secret. As Brian and I have known for many years, the secret is this: it's less about building a better mousetrap and more about selling and marketing the mousetrap you already have.

Like my financial planner, your business undoubtedly provides much more lasting value than the Pet Rock. But if you don't understand the power of marketing and haven't expended sufficient effort in strengthening this leg of your business stool, it doesn't matter how great your *mousetrap* is.

Finding the Right Marketing Strategy

Sales & Marketing must be the primary focus of any small business. But how should you market your service or product? Which marketing strategy will be most effective, most efficient and most profitable? Let's investigate two different marketing strategies: Transactional Marketing and Relational Marketing. Then you decide which one seems best.

Transactional Marketing

With a Transactional Marketing approach, small-business owners spend most of their energy finding their next customers. When they get a customer, the focus is on providing their services, getting paid and then looking for the next customer. They become so preoccupied with finding the next customer that they don't stay in contact with the person or business they have just served. Every day is a new day, and there is no link to the past work they've done or the relationships they've already established.

In other words, a Transactional Marketing approach takes all your time, energy and money, and all you get for your efforts is a one-time transaction. The customer is choosing you because of convenience or price. You feel no connection to them, and they feel no loyalty towards you. Once the client is found, you receive no additional value for your marketing efforts.

> *Sales & Marketing must be the primary focus of any small business.*

Coupons, newspaper ads, promotional pieces, random mailings, buying lists of *guaranteed* leads, Internet leads, blast e-mail messages and promotional websites are all examples of transactional methods. Customers who find you through Transactional Marketing strategies can be hit or miss. They can be demanding, uncooperative and very price-conscious because there has been no trust or connection made other than the transaction between your business and them. It's okay to find customers through advertising, but you'll want to develop business relationships with these clients to create repeat customers and ultimately advocates for your business.

Early on in my career, I learned that just having transactional relationships with customers was unsatisfying both personally and professionally. One day I got a phone call from a prospective buyer, Tom, who had seen a newspaper ad for one of my home listings. Trying to set up an appointment with Tom was a challenge and once he viewed the home, he decided he didn't like it. Even though Tom said he was committed to buying a house, he wasn't eager for assistance from me. He didn't want to share his phone number or any pertinent information. He was always guarded and answered curtly when I suggested strategies for looking for his ideal home. Tom also admitted that he was talking to other Realtors and crosschecking information he received from each. Our working relationship was strained at best.

Believe it or not, Tom finally did purchase a home through me. After the property closed, I felt like Tom and I both needed a long vacation. I was exhausted from trying to show Tom that I was competent in my field and truly had his best interests at heart. I don't know if he ever really trusted me. The entire experience was a tug of war.

Transactional marketing always seems to generate clients similar to Tom. This type of relationship actually hinders you from building your business by requiring the unnecessary depletion of your three precious resources—time, energy and money.

Relational Marketing:
The Working by Referral Approach

In contrast to Transactional Marketing, Relational Marketing is based on small-business owners maintaining a consistent level of contact with, and care for, the people in their databases (which we'll explore later), leading to a steady stream of repeat and referred clients. In other words, with a Relational Marketing approach, all your time, energy and money are invested in relationships. Getting referrals from people who know who you are, what you do and who trust you results in prospective clients who already recognize your value.

> *With a Relational Marketing approach, all your time, energy and money are invested in relationships.*

The Relational (Working by Referral) approach produces both a current *and* future payout. In the present, you will enjoy high-quality leads and a steady income. And with each transaction, you build relationships with people who will continue to send you referrals in the months and years to come.

I'm hoping you've had the opportunity to serve customers who were referred to you, maybe from a family member or friend. Most likely these people were a pleasure to work with because they trusted you. They were serious about using your service, became loyal to you and were happy to pay you for the value you brought.

A great example of how a business can transition from Transactional to Relational Marketing is the story of Pioneer Basement in Massachusetts, owned by Steve Andras. Steve pioneered a method of waterproofing basements so that they stay dry permanently. But although he had been in business 26 years, Steve was still spending as much as $80,000 a month advertising his business to find customers. Now that we've taught Steve how to work by referral, his business has grown by 65 percent even though he has reduced his monthly advertising costs to just $10,000. The quality of the customers he typically works with today is higher because they come by way of referral, and there's an established level of trust and connection the first time they meet. Increasing revenue, reducing expenses and improving the quality of your customers are powerful examples of how this Big Idea for Small Business can bring about great results.

> *The quality of the lead you generate is directly related to the source from which it comes.*

Having used both Transactional Marketing and the Working by Referral approach myself, I can confirm one thing without a doubt: the quality of the lead you generate is directly related to the source from which it comes.

You can opt for a *cold* low-quality lead, spending time, money and energy to find that one random client who may or may not turn into a challenging customer. Or you can receive a *warm* high-quality lead referred by someone you know who will likely become an enjoyable, loyal customer. If you want your business filled with the latter, then our Working by Referral system can deliver those leads in spades.

> *Working by Referral is a disciplined and systematic way to generate a steady stream of high-quality leads from people you already know.*

Working by Referral is a disciplined and systematic way to generate a steady stream of high-quality leads from people you already know. It focuses on the Big Idea for Small Business and capitalizes on generating leads from your existing relationships so you don't have to reinvent your business anew each day. But in order to have your name at the forefront of people's minds when they're thinking about buying your product or service, you need to develop the primary tool of Working by Referral: a database.

From Names to Relationships

A database is not simply a list of names, phone numbers and addresses; that's a phone book. Rather, a database is a list of relationships. If you've just started your business, you may think a database will take years to create. But you'll see that you can generate a working database in just a few days. People who have been in business for years may assume they already have a database. But if you haven't been intentional and strategic about developing and maintaining that database, all you really have is a list of past customers.

A database is a list of relationships.

The intrinsic value of a small business lies in the loyalty of its customers. When doctors, dentists, attorneys or accountants sell their businesses, buyers are purchasing their databases of repeat and referral customers. Building a database is ultimately how you move your business from a Transactional to a Relational approach.

Going for the Gold

When I give seminars to businesspeople today, I challenge them to make a list of all the people they know. Typically, they'll spend 30 minutes compiling a list of 20 names.

"Good," I say. "Now think of 20 more."

In another 45 minutes, their list is longer. I prompt them to add another 20 names to it, reminding them not to forget the owner of the dry cleaner they see every other Saturday or the mechanic who fixes their car. When I first put together my own database in 1988, I distinctly remember compiling a list with 86 names on it. Making that list was like throwing a rock into a pond and watching the ripples spread out as one name led to another.

Here are a few suggestions to help you start building your database:

▶ Family

▶ Friends

▶ Neighbors

▶ High school classmates

▶ College alumni

▶ Teams/clubs with whom you're associated

▶ Services you use: landscaper, dry cleaner, baker, etc.

▶ Past clients

▶ Current clients

▶ Groups and associations

▶ Other small-business owners

▶ Business associates and networks

If you're in a professional service industry, The Mayor Campaign Dialog (see *www.takincareofbusiness.biz*) is a simple dialog you can use to help determine whether a potential relationship is appropriate to add to your database.

A Hard-Working Database

> *The intrinsic value of a small business lies in the loyalty of its customers.*

In 1994, I put the Working by Referral system and my database to the test when I went on vacation with my sister Terry. We were both single at the time and needed a break from working hard. Terry took control of planning the trip, and I was stunned when she announced that we were going to

Australia—*for five weeks*. When I protested that I couldn't possibly be away from the office for that long, she countered, "Too late, the trip's already booked."

So off we went and had a great time touring Australia. The payoff? When we returned, I had 37 referred leads waiting for me like the morning newspaper on the doorstep. And many of those leads turned into transactions!

Target Marketing:
Sorting and Qualifying Your Database

So if a database of 100 names is good, wouldn't one with 1,000 names be even better? Not necessarily. You don't strike oil by digging a mile wide and just an inch below the surface; you've got to dig deep. The goal is not to have the biggest database but to have one that delivers results. To make your business big, your focus needs to be small.

Sorting and qualifying your database is a form of Target Marketing. Target Marketing is when a company aims its marketing efforts at a specific group of customers. A well-defined target market is the first element of a powerful marketing strategy. This type of marketing is the most effective and efficient way to focus your finite resources of time, energy and money.

> *A well-defined target market is the first element of a powerful marketing strategy.*

Everyone has to use his or her limited resources wisely. And business owners have to focus these resources on those individuals who are likely to use them in future transactions or who will refer others to them. You may have heard of the Pareto Principle, named after the Italian economist Vilfredo Pareto, who observed that 20 percent of the people in Italy owned 80 percent of the country's wealth. Pareto's so-called *80–20 Rule* came to be applied to business, creating such accepted maxims as 80 percent of sales are generated by 20 percent of clients. I've found that the Pareto Principle also rings true in the Working by Referral system: 20 percent of the people in your database will generate 80 percent of your referrals.

Of course this isn't a hard-and-fast rule, but it illustrates the importance of ranking the names in your database with the grades A, B, C or D so you spend your resources where the payoff is the greatest. Remember, a database is not a mailing list; it's a list of relationships. You should have a relationship with everyone in your database and they should recognize your name instantly when you contact them.

Now it's time to sort your database by the quality of each relationship. I've found that in business as well as in life, the closer the relationship, the more time you want to spend with that person. Those at the top of your database will be the people to whom you give your greatest attention. Here's how to categorize the names in your database:

The people who send you multiple referrals: A+

These folks are your ravin' advocates. They love you and think they are doing people a favor by referring them to you. Mostly, these will be customers who have experienced your exemplary service and skill firsthand.

People most likely to refer to you: A

These are people who haven't made multiple referrals to you yet, but it's just a matter of time before they do. Family members, good friends and happy clients belong here.

People who would refer to you if asked and shown how: B

Neighbors or acquaintances with whom you share a common interest—parents of your children's classmates, members of your church, people you see at your garden-club meetings—should be ranked with a B. They may not yet know that you have your own business, so as you build relationships with them, tell them what you do and that you would be happy to have their referrals.

People who might refer to you in the future: C

C people are in the infancy stage of a relationship with you. They are people you are hoping to get to know better.

People to be deleted from your database: D

These are customers who are demanding and difficult. It takes energy to be around them, and when you see their names on caller ID, you don't pick up the phone. Deleting these names from your database is empowering—even if you're desperate for business. As crazy as it sounds, go ahead and do it. No matter how much time and energy you spend with these people, they aren't going to advance your business or send you referrals.

Now it's Your Turn

Take enough time to really think about the people in your database before you assign them a letter. Remember, you are not grading people on how much you like or dislike them. You are just determining who will best be able to generate the referrals that will make your business grow.

Sam & Edith's Story:
Hitting the Target

Sam and Edith Elzie's story is a classic example of how a database can help your business go from Transactional to Relational.

Sam and Edith attended their first Turning Point in 1996. They had 440 names, addresses and phone numbers in what they called a database, but it was really just a glorified mailing list. Over the course of the previous 12 months, they had closed just 13 real estate transactions.

They began working with one of Buffini & Company's Business Coaches, Roibin McFarling. He encouraged them to think of their mailing list not as a whole, but in terms of the quality of the relationships inside it. Who were their favorite people? Who were their most valued customers? Who referred them most? Who was most likely to refer them in the future?

As they called through their client list, they spoke with people who had no idea who they were. They also sorted the names into A, B and C categories and deleted the D names. They then began giving their very best clients and contacts more attention and applied many of the marketing tactics you'll hear about in the coming chapters.

Just one year later, Sam and Edith received 308 referrals from the same database that had produced just 13 sales the year before. And after 15 years of Working by Referral, they were able to sell their business in Bear, Delaware. The Big Idea for Small Business allowed Sam and Edith to sell their business and fulfill a dream retirement.

Now that you know how to build your database and identify key relationships, it's time to focus your efforts on systematically targeting those relationships. In the next chapter, you will discover the tools to generate more opportunity and grow your business.

CHAPTER **FOUR**

Takin' Care of
Sales

Joe Niego

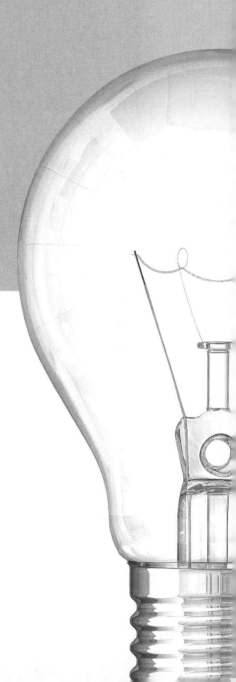

*Pretend that every single person you meet has
a sign around his or her neck that says, "Make
me feel important." Not only will you succeed
in sales, you will succeed in life.*

– Mary Kay Ash

Takin' Care of Sales

Joe Niego

Two men were hiking in the mountains in Colorado, enjoying the majestic Rocky Mountain scenery and experiencing the calm that the early morning brings. As they rounded a bend in the trail, they were quickly reminded of another reality of nature. Straight ahead, in the middle of their path, were an enormous grizzly bear and her two cubs. The two hikers immediately stopped and began to retreat slowly, hoping the grizzly would leave them alone. Unfortunately, they had moved too far into her territory. Feeling threatened, the bear lunged toward them.

The two men turned and began to run, leaping over fallen trees and dodging saplings as they headed off the trail and into the woods. They could hear the bear behind them, crashing through the underbrush and gaining on them.

With the angry grizzly hot on their tail, one of the hikers suddenly stopped, pulled a pair of running shoes out of his backpack, and began lacing them up.

The other man cried out in a panic, "What are you doing? Do you really think you can outrun the grizzly with those?" The hiker calmly looked at his companion and replied, "No. I don't have to outrun the grizzly. I just have to outrun you!"

Our recent business climate is similar to what those two hikers encountered. One minute we were enjoying a booming economic market and then, abruptly it seemed, we were face-to-face with a fierce *grizzly* market that threatened the very existence of our business. And many business owners are still fighting for their lives.

It's time to stop, think strategically and lace up your running shoes. You need to acquire the tools necessary to survive any challenging market and outrun the competition. In this chapter you will learn a strategy to build upon the database you have sorted and qualified. You'll discover the Three C's to Success—Contact, Care and Community—and how to blend them into your business systems to generate high-quality referrals. This strategy makes the Big Idea for Small Business come to life; it keeps your business ahead of the bear. Next time someone asks, "How is your business?" you won't have to say, "It's a bear!"

CONTACT: Making it Meaningful

There are plenty of marketing gimmicks that claim to keep your name foremost in potential clients' minds. I've certainly tried many of them. One year I mailed out baseball schedules for the Chicago Cubs and the White Sox. The next year I sent out football schedules for the Bears. Other people regularly send out magnetic calendars, jar openers and ice scrapers—along with everyone else who is trying to sell a service. But these items fail to communicate the essence of the services you provide and your expertise.

In our first book, "Work by Referral. Live the Good Life!," many readers told us the story of Mary P. resonated with them because they could see themselves in her. Mary is a real estate professional who thought she had found the perfect strategy for maintaining contact with her past clients. For more than a decade, she had sent them recipe cards on a monthly basis. One day, when a former client called to say, "I was thinking of you the other day," Mary silently praised her marketing strategy for doing its job. But the client's next words cut her to the quick. "We just sold our house and bought another, and I wanted to give you our new address so you could continue sending me those wonderful recipe cards!"

In that moment, Mary realized her recipe cards hadn't done a thing to generate referrals and repeat business from clients. "People thought of me as the lady who likes to bake, not as a real estate professional to help with their family's real estate needs," said Mary. "All that work of sending out cards for 10 years; I was devastated."

Although Mary's recipes had been appreciated, they hadn't demonstrated her professionalism. Consequently, the people in Mary's database remembered her culinary interest, not her skill as a Realtor.

At Buffini & Company, we emphasize maintaining *Contact* with your clients through three different channels in order to demonstrate your professional competence and personal character: Items of Value, eReports and Outgoing Calls.

Items of Value

Buffini & Company has devoted considerable effort to developing what we term Items of Value to remind people in your database *who* you are, *what* you do and *why* they can trust you. Unlike baseball schedules or recipe cards, which emphasize the sender and the sale, Items of Value are single-topic newsletters focused on the recipients and their personal concerns. The message shifts from "Buy from me!" to "Here's an Item of Value for you." At the same time, the Items of Value remind clients that you have the competence they are seeking while also keeping you at the forefront of their minds.

Here are some examples of Items of Value that we've shared with many of our customers:

▶ How to Protect Yourself from Identity Theft

▶ Are Your Energy Bills Too High?

▶ Top Ten Tax Tips

▶ How to Raise Your Credit Score

▶ Budget or Busted – Top Ways You Can Save, Today!

Visit *www.takincareofbusiness.biz* to view sample Items of Value.

eReports

An eReport is an Item of Value delivered via e-mail. One of the benefits of an eReport is that it makes it easy for your customers to respond. "I appreciate receiving the information you send me every month," is a common reply sent from clients who receive an eReport in their inbox.

Visit *www.takincareofbusiness.biz* to view sample eReports.

Outgoing Calls

The telephone is one of the quickest and most efficient ways to directly contact a large number of people. Due to its real-time response, cold-calling has historically been the preferred sales tool for many industries, such as insurance companies, financial planners and stockbrokers. With the advent of the *Do Not Call Implementation Act* of 2003, many small businesses lost their source of new leads. The act is intended to protect consumers from receiving unsolicited phone calls from people they did not have a prior relationship with or had not done business with in the previous 18 months.

> *The telephone is one of the quickest and most efficient ways to directly contact a large number of people.*

Fortunately, the law did not affect our marketing strategy. The Working by Referral marketing system never promoted cold-calling. When you call people in your database, you're calling people with whom you have a relationship. You're not calling people you don't know. When you properly execute the Referral Systems, people tend to be more open to hearing from you.

Here's the approach we recommend; after sending an Item of Value in the mail or an eReport electronically, make a brief call to the recipient and say something like this:

> *Hi (name), this is Joe Niego. I just wanted to check in with you and see how you are doing. (Engage in conversation by asking questions about him or her.) The other reason I'm calling is that I recently came across some information stating that identify theft is the #1 fraud in North America today. There are some recommended steps you can take to protect yourself and your family from this type of fraud. I just want to make sure you and all my favorite customers are protected as much as possible.*
>
> *Oh, by the way (name)…, I'm never too busy for any of your referrals.*

We recommend that you maintain regular contact with the people in your database by sending an Item of Value via mail at the beginning of the month, sending an eReport in the middle of each month and following up each piece with a phone call.

In training thousands of small-business owners over the last decade, I was not surprised to discover that many have *call reluctance*. In other words, they get paralyzed worrying what to say and are afraid of being perceived as *pushy* or *bothersome*. When business owners tell me they have a fear of the phone, I'll ask, "Have you ever been attacked by one?" The truth is, most people enjoy conversations with somebody they have a relationship with. The key concept of Working by Referral is that every interaction deepens the relationships you have with your clients.

CARE: Adding a Personal Touch

Rhetoric about the exemplary care people will receive when they become customers is standard in many businesses. Sometimes those words become reality, but all too often actions don't live up to promises. That's because many business owners are distracted by continually thinking about where they are going to find their next customers or transactions. But when you only focus on completing a transaction and moving on to the next one, your clients may feel deserted and forgotten. Your opportunity to receive referrals from them vanishes.

You can, however, make your clients feel cared for by staying in touch with them in two specific ways: personal notes and Pop-Bys.

Personal Notes

The most powerful and least expensive way to deepen a relationship with a client is to send a handwritten personal note—a rare find in anyone's mailbox these days.

Personal notes represent true value to your customers. Surrounded by so much slick direct-mail advertising, computerized phone messages and mass e-mails, people really appreciate the human connection and intimacy that a handwritten note conveys.

> *The most powerful and least expensive way to deepen a relationship with a client is to send a handwritten personal note.*

A handwritten note will always get read. I can't imagine tossing one in the trash can without opening it. And neither will your customers. Yes, writing notes does take time. But if you're consistent about carving out a small amount of time every day to write them, the task won't consume you. Keep a stack of note cards and envelopes on your desk. Each morning before you check your e-mail messages, write a pre-determined number of notes. Three notes a day adds up to 15 a week or 60 a month. Imagine making 60 meaningful impressions on your customer base every month!

The message from a handwritten note lingers, unlike an e-mail message that is often quickly deleted. A good note isn't about expressing yourself. It's about listening to your customers and writing something that will resonate with their needs, challenges, hurts or desires. Go to *www.takincareofbusiness.biz* for examples of personal notes that Brian and I have written.

Last fall, Brian and I were on stage presenting our Turning Point event in my hometown of Chicago. My mother attended the event and sat through two days of content even though she is retired and not looking to start a new business. She was there to support me. A few days later, I received a touching, handwritten note authored by my mother. As you can imagine, it made my day. Even though I've accomplished many things in life and traveled the world with Brian speaking to hundreds of thousands of people each year, it was amazing how this personal note from my mom affected me.

> *Never underestimate the power of a personal note. Sometimes the message is just what someone needs to hear that day.*

> Dear Joe,
>
> Just wanted to drop you a short note to let you know how great a public speaker you are becoming.
>
> It was great to see you in action once again up on the stage. You and Brian are a dynamic duo. I'm so proud of all your accomplishments. I'm more proud of you as my wonderful and successful son.
>
> Love, Mom

Never underestimate the power of a personal note. Sometimes the message is just what someone needs to hear that day.

Pop-Bys

Staying in contact with people is key to Working by Referral. A Pop-By is a method we use to stay connected on a face-to-face basis. Unlike a personal note, a Pop-By is interactive. You get a chance to look into a person's eyes, shake his or her hand and ask how he or she is doing.

And since 75 percent of all communication is nonverbal, you can convey much more in a Pop-By than you can in a personal note. By your mere presence, a Pop-By communicates that you value the relationship and care enough to invest your time on a visit.

Doing a Pop-By is easy: visit your favorite people in your database and bring them a simple token of appreciation. You can easily adapt Pop-Bys to the season or holiday. For example, the week before Mother's Day, drop by with a small bouquet of flowers or a potted plant. Imagine the joy!

One word of caution: give of who you are, not of what you have. Don't agonize over your Pop-By choice. It is simply a small token of appreciation. The biggest gift is *your time and attention*. Your effort in taking the time to Pop-By will be more valued than any gift.

For more Pop-By gift ideas, go to *www.takincareofbusiness.biz*.

COMMUNITY: Creating a Client for Life

In 2000, public policy expert Robert D. Putnam published one of the most discussed books of recent times, "Bowling Alone: The Collapse and Revival of American Community." Putnam examines the trend of Americans becoming more solitary, as evidenced by declining memberships in clubs, unions, churches and volunteer activities. Over the past quarter century, the number of people attending club meetings has dropped 58 percent, entertaining friends at home has diminished by 45 percent and a third fewer families report sharing regular family dinners.

Business transactions have also radically changed. Most business deals 25 years ago were made face-to-face, providing plenty of opportunities for personal contact and free exchange of ideas. But today our interactions are more virtual than social, as e-mail, video conferencing and the Internet have replaced meetings and phone calls.

But even though so many of us may be *bowling alone,* we still crave community. Witness the tremendous growth of social networking sites like Facebook and LinkedIn, which have attracted millions of users. This clearly demonstrates individuals' hard-wired desire to connect, but it also serves as a reminder that the age-old places of connection are not satisfying the needs of people any longer. For example, people today have a hard time meeting one another, which has resulted in the incredible growth of dating websites.

Small-business owners are in an excellent position to restore some of the connectedness that has become so lacking. By hosting social events, you can create a vibrant community network with the people in your database, strengthen relationships and build loyalty. Your clients' lives will be richer for it and so will your business. In fact, fostering community is essential to your business.

> *Like any personal relationship, the greater contact you have with the people in your database, the stronger their bonds will be with you.*

Like any personal relationship, the greater contact you have with the people in your database, the stronger their bonds will be with you. Think about the concept of breaking bread and how significant it is to building relationships. The major holidays like Thanksgiving, Hanukkah, Christmas and Easter are always centered on a great meal and family celebration. Likewise, three of the following four strategies for building your client community involve breaking bread together: client breakfasts, a cup of joe and client parties. The fourth strategy, Client Communities Online, is not centered around food, but it can help put food on your table!

Client Breakfasts

Taking a client to breakfast creates an opportunity to build community in your database, one relationship at a time. And according to nutrition experts, breakfast is the most important meal of the day. It's a win-win! Breakfast is the easiest meal to fit into any day. Usually, as the day progresses, schedules change, appointments run late and emergencies arise. By committing to breakfast, however, there are fewer obstacles to get in the way. It's a cost-effective way to stay healthy and build your business at the same time. Two eggs over easy, a short stack of pan-cakes, two strips of bacon and great conversation with an A+ client—I can't think of a better way to start the day.

Client Coffees

Have you ever wanted to get together with someone, but gathering for a meal required too much of a time commitment? Meeting for coffee with a client doesn't require reservations or a big time commitment, and it doesn't break your pocketbook. It's short and sweet, allows for flexibility and is an ideal way to make a deposit into the relational bank account. A cup of joe is a great idea!

Annual Client Appreciation Parties

Client parties allow you to give generously to those in your database and make it more comfortable to ask for referrals later. Your parties will also provide a chance for folks to inter-act with other like-minded people, which means they'll have a great experience, too.

You're in the business of generating leads.

I use a party to deepen the connection with my clients as well as other relationships I've developed through my business. This is typically an annual event designed to thank them for their support, continuing patronage and referrals. I opt for a Fourth of July party, which dovetails with our company's practice of distributing 16,000 American flags throughout the neighborhood. The party is a lot of fun and generates referrals for us each year.

If you would like to see pictures from my Client Appreciation Party, go to *www.takincareofbusiness.biz*.

Client Communities Online

Since the late 1990s, the Internet has gained popularity and people have discovered the convenience and power of having immediate access to information, products and services. For example, according to *Search Engine Journal*:

▸ 89 percent of consumers shop online for Christmas gifts.

▸ 60 percent of individuals search for coupons and specials before going shopping.

▸ 75 percent of patients research symptoms online before discussing them with a doctor.

▸ One out of every five couples who got married last year met online first.

Over the past 20-plus years, technology has changed our culture—especially in the way we interact and connect. And it will continue to advance at an even more rapid pace in the years to come. The principles of our Working by Referral system are timeless, however, and are as relevant today as they were yesterday and will be tomorrow. If anything, technology gives small-business owners an additional opportunity to connect with customers and build their business in a relational way.

Technology gives small-business owners an additional opportunity to connect with customers and build their business in a relational way.

Whether you post customer feedback surveys on your website, leverage Facebook so customers can interact with one another or use Twitter to enhance your customers' understanding or appreciation of your product or service, you are providing value, connecting with customers and deepening your relationship with them.

Keep That Referral Point of View

I can hear some of you saying now, "Hey, my main business is accounting, insurance or financial services. But these guys want me to become my city's social director!" We understand your concern. But remember the Big Idea for Small Business: you're in the business of generating leads. And if you want to succeed, you need to dedicate time every day to the lead generation strategies of Contact, Care and Community.

Right now you may be wondering how the Three C's will lead to greater freedom in your life when you have to make time to write notes, make personal visits and host parties. The good news is that once you establish the Three C's as part of your business system, nurturing the people in your database will take much less time than starting over every day trying to drum up new business.

Unlike the many hours you now spend hunting for leads or trying to serve poor-quality leads, the time it takes to incorporate the Three C's into your business is manageable and under your control. The key, however, is to apply all three elements consistently.

In the next chapter, you'll learn how to make the Three C's a daily discipline in your business. As a result, the people who are the recipients of your Contact, Care and Community will be generating quality leads for you while you're working with your current clients. Suddenly, you'll find your business continuing to grow while you are living your life.

Irving's Story:
The Long, Caring Arm of the Law

Irving Hymson is the principle owner of the law firm Hymson Goldstein & Pantiliat, P.L.L.C., in Scottsdale, Arizona. For years, the firm had no marketing program but wanted to increase its clients. "Sure, we would run a few advertisements every once in a while to make us feel like we were doing something 'effective,' but they never yielded a significant number of new clients," said Irving. With no consistent communication with their existing clients, the firm had few referral sources.

Working with Buffini & Company Leadership Coach Ward Harrington, Irving concentrated on building a database (using the Mayor Campaign to generate names), writing personal notes ("The minute I hang up the phone with a prospective client or receive an e-mail"), making phone calls to former clients and sending Items of Value. The first year of using the Working by Referral methods, Irving generated 119 referrals. The second year his referrals numbered 172. The third year he had 312 referrals. And for many years his referrals have continued to be significant. This year he believes he'll generate an even greater number of referrals whether the economic climate is good or bad. The system has worked so well for him that his entire law firm uses it, with great results.

"We have experienced new business in excess of high seven figures that is directly attributable to the Working by Referral system," said Irving. "Our firm has doubled in size and continues to grow even though our advertising has dropped to almost nil." Greater referrals are only one side of the story, though. The quality of Irving's clients has also enhanced his law practice. "Most people think that a visit to a lawyer is just a notch above a visit to the dentist," said Irving. "We have found that when clients come to us by referral, their attitude is entirely different. They expect that we'll put their interests first and will be on their side for the long haul, rather than assume we view them as simply more revenue for the firm. When clients believe we care for them, they help us achieve our mission statement, which is to restore the attorney to the traditional role as the trusted family and business advisor. That is why we are proud to say, *'Our Business Is Your Peace of Mind.'*"

CHAPTER FIVE

Daily Disciplines for
The Big Idea

Joe Niego

*Discipline yourself to do the things you
need to do when you need to do them,
and the day will come when you will
be able to do the things you want to do
when you want to do them.*

– Zig Ziglar

Daily Disciplines for the Big Idea

Joe Niego

For the want of a nail, the horseshoe was lost. For the want of a horseshoe, a horse was lost. For the want of a horse, the rider was lost. For the want of a rider, the message was lost. For the want of a message, the battle was lost. For the want of a battle, the war was lost. For the want of a war, the kingdom was lost. And all for the want of a horseshoe's nail.

– Author unknown

The earliest reference to this proverb dates back to the death of Richard III of England at the battle of Bosworth Field. In the story, King Richard famously shouted, "A horse, a horse. My kingdom for a horse!" as depicted in Shakespeare's play *Richard III*, circa 1591.

It was true almost 500 years ago and it'll be true 500 years from now that executing on the small details of business makes the difference between success and failure. So what details do we believe are critical? Yes, it's nice to have a clean desk, but that's not essential. Yes, it's fun to work on the design of brochures, signs, cards or websites, but they won't create a steady stream of customers. This chapter will lay out the essential daily disciplines you need to follow to achieve the Big Idea for Small Business and to ensure your business won't be lost for the want of customers.

Caution: There Are No Shortcuts to Generating Leads

In 1967, Amana introduced the *Radarange.* For $495 (approximately $3,200 in today's money), you could buy the first consumer microwave oven. This product forever changed our culture. No longer did you have to wait an appropriate amount of time for food to cook; you could get results in a fraction of the time. This microwave mentality has now spread to taking care of our bodies with promises of *six-minute abs,* or *lose 40 pounds in 40 days.* It also permeates our financial outlook with lures of becoming an *instant millionaire* or *overnight success.*

Both Brian and I have come to the conclusion that a formula for an on-the-spot business transformation does not exist. Anything touted as a *quick fix* will likely result in dashed expectations when success doesn't materialize. Time is necessary to build a profitable business. Executing the Working by Referral system requires that you be disciplined in your approach.

> *The only way to make lasting and successful change is to foster winning habits.*

The only way to make lasting and successful change is to foster winning habits. And the single most important habit for a small-business owner is to systematically execute simple lead-generation disciplines *every single workday.* Naturally, there will be days when you simply can't find the time or energy to generate leads. Our advice, however, is to make this the exception to the rule.

Most businesses have ebbs and flows related to business cycles. Some months it's all you can do to manage the clients you have, while during slower periods you worry that starting your own business was pure folly. While you have to accept a certain amount of turbulence in running your own business, it's crucial that you don't let anxiety or fear sidetrack you. If you neglect making calls, writing notes and doing Pop-Bys during the rough patches, first you'll lose one day, then another, and soon you'll have lost several weeks. Suddenly, you have even fewer clients and all because you took your eye off the prize.

Vince Lombardi, the famed coach of the Green Bay Packers, knew something about the rewards of practicing good habits. "Winning is not a *sometime* thing; it's an *all* time thing," he said. "You don't win once in a while, you don't do things right once in a while, you do them right all the time. Winning is habit. Unfortunately, so is losing."

Here are the disciplines you need to develop to generate leads on a consistent basis.

DAILY DISCIPLINE #1: Understanding Your *Why*

The daily grind of business can wear you down. Regain drive and focus by identifying the *Why* behind your daily routine. Having a goal for doing a Pop-By, dealing with a transaction challenge or hosting a business party gives these activities a clear purpose. Focusing on your goals and what they mean to you and your family brings new passion to those often-mundane tasks of lead generation. Your goals are the *Why*.

If you find yourself tempted to skip lead-generation activities one day, think about how your choice will impact your goals. At our seminars, Brian and I have helped more than 2 million people articulate their goals, and we have received thousands of notes from business owners who have shared how their goals keep them focused on staying disciplined and bring meaning to their work. What are your goals? Are they in writing? Do you think about them daily?

Nancy M. came to the Turning Point in Chicago in 1997. A single mother of four kids, she worked hard every day in her real estate business to provide for her family. Although she always managed to pay her bills, she was unable to provide many of the niceties and special extras her kids asked for. During the event, Nancy laid out a series of goals. One of those goals in particular became her *Why*. Her children had asked many times to visit Disney World, but over the years had resigned themselves to the fact that this dream would not come true. Nancy's goal was to take all four of her children, their best friends, and a few parents to help chaperone on a two-week vacation to Disney

World—all expenses paid. Fourteen months later, 16 children and three adults spent two weeks in the happiest place on earth all paid for by a woman on a mission. She was more diligent and focused on her business during that time than at any other period. Nancy generated three times the volume of leads she typically did in a year because her *Why* was so clear. The Big Idea for Small Business proved to be a big deal for Nancy and her family.

> *Setting clear goals is imperative to staying focused and on task.*

Setting clear goals is imperative to staying focused and on task. You must have a written set of short-, mid- and long-range goals for yourself, for your business and for your life. It is imperative that you put your goals in writing and that you read them frequently. Your goals are the *Why,* the Big Idea is your *What* and the Working by Referral system is your *How.*

For resources on setting short-, mid- and long-range goals, go to *www.takincareofbusiness.biz.*

DAILY DISCIPLINE #2: Structure Your Workday

Part of the appeal of owning a business is being able to choose the hours you work. But that very freedom can also contribute to the demise of your business. Without a structured workday, it's all too easy to get sidetracked from the vital activities your company needs in order to grow. It's easy to focus on the less important but more urgent distractions instead.

> *Without a structured workday, it's all too easy to get sidetracked from the vital activities your company needs in order to grow.*

Early in my career I discovered that the more structured my day, the more freedom and flexibility I experienced. That's not as contradictory as it sounds. By scheduling the important activities into my day, I actually worked fewer hours than when I was scrambling to fit these tasks in at the end of the day. Simultaneously, these scheduled activities also produced the treasured referrals I sought.

Let me give you a few suggestions to help you structure your day:

Schedule Your Start and End Times:

Establishing a consistent time to start your day is one of the most productive things you can do. For me, that time is 8:30 a.m. The time doesn't have to be early; it just needs to be scheduled.

Establishing a definitive end time to your day is also crucial. There have probably been many days when you've left the office feeling guilty that you left a task undone. Leave anyway. There will always be a call to make, a challenge to address or a report to run. Remember that you work to achieve your goals—not to maintain a 24/7 work schedule. As an added benefit, you will find that if you impose a strict deadline on the tasks you have to do, you'll work more diligently during your day.

Use Time-Blocking for Lead-Generation Activities:

Scheduling uninterrupted time to execute lead-generating activities like making calls, writing notes and doing Pop-Bys is non-negotiable; it must be done. You can be flexible about when you schedule your time block, but just make sure you do it daily.

I schedule a *power hour* in the morning and one in the afternoon. By remaining focused and diligent during each of these hours, I can then take a 30-minute break afterwards. I'm always amazed by how much can be accomplished in one focused hour, which, ultimately, allows me to work less. Freedom follows only when you make productivity your first priority.

Take a Break:

In his best-selling book, "The Power of Full Engagement," Tony Schwartz states that the ability to rest and recover from intense mental activity is the key to high performance. There are normal ebbs and flows within a day, and it is extremely difficult to be 100 percent productive all day long. Work hard, then schedule a break. Make sure you also stop for lunch—not only for a necessary break, but also for your health. Leisurely lunches are fine now and then, but schedule them so they don't become a daily event. Long lunches are poor habits that slowly creep into a small-business owner's day, so schedule your lunch times and stick to them.

Containing Customer Service:

Customer Service is your *job*, but Sales & Marketing is your *business*. Serving customers can consume your entire day if you allow it. Be proactive and schedule a specific time to make all customer-related calls. When you proactively handle Customer Service issues, the phone call lasts two minutes. When the customer initiates the call and you're forced to react, the conversation can stretch to 20 minutes and you'll be defensive the whole time. If you can't get in touch with your customer, leave a detailed message and ask for a detailed message in return.

DAILY DISCIPLINE #3: Create a Personal Business Standard

Have you ever come home at the end of a long day feeling beat up and tired but not sure what you accomplished? That's because we often spend our days putting out fires—dealing with the glitch in the computer system, making time to see the salesperson who came calling, or ordering supplies that are on the verge of running out. Often the only way we gauge whether or not we've had a good day is if we've billed an adequate amount.

> *The best way to measure the effectiveness of your day is to have a Personal Business Standard.*

Very few small businesses turn a profit 365 days a year, so we must also measure our success by the daily activities we accomplish. The best way to measure the effectiveness of your day is to have a Personal Business Standard, which is a tool that allows you to set a daily goal for the lead-generating activities you want to execute. Thousands of entrepreneurs in our Business Coaching program earn sizable incomes by holding themselves accountable to a Personal Business Standard like the one laid out in the Win-the-Day Formula on page 63.

DAILY DISCIPLINE #4: Do It Now

I've seen many business owners paralyzed by perfectionism. Wanting to do a task flawlessly, they never get beyond the first step. Of course you want to do a good job, but you have to do it in the time that's available to you.

Newer business owners are especially plagued with paralysis by analysis. Often they are indecisive and unproductive because they feel they don't have the experience or knowledge to take action. But they can't gain experience or knowledge if they never take action!

This is business; not brain surgery. If you make a mistake, nobody is going to die, including you. Making mistakes and failing are common steps on the road to success. And if you are a veteran business owner stuck on a production plateau, you have to make a break with your usual business methods in order to achieve better results. In short, you must take action.

> *Making mistakes and failing are common steps on the road to success.*

Although there never seems to be a perfect time to make a call to a potential client, call anyway. You may feel the Item of Value you are giving to your clients isn't quite right for everyone. But give it anyway. You may never write notes to clients that they'll treasure forever. But write them anyway. Just do it!

DAILY DISCIPLINE #5: Seize the Day

One of my all-time favorite movie scenes is in the 1989 film *Dead Poets Society*. I love the unorthodox teaching style of the lead character, John Keating, brilliantly played by Robin Williams. Keating has his class of high school boys stand in the school hallway overlooking the trophy case, where he draws their attention to the picture of students who graduated 100 years earlier. These former students walked the same hallways, sat in the same classrooms and studied the same subjects. Now, Keating says, these people are fertilizing daffodils. Listen closely, he says, as they bequeath their legacy to you. *"Carpe diem,"* he whispers, "Seize the day!"

> *As small and insignificant as one day may seem to your business, it really is the difference between winning and losing.*

The psychology behind harnessing daily disciplines is based on understanding the importance of each individual day. Often we falter in achieving goals because we fail to appreciate that small steps add up to big results. As small and insignificant as one day may seem to your business, it really is the difference between winning and losing. Robert Collier, author of self-help and New Thought metaphysical books in the 20th century, once said, "If you think you are too small to make a difference, you have never gone to bed with a mosquito."

The value of a single day is often lost when an individual feels overwhelmed. But each day you follow the disciplines of lead generation equates to one nail in the shoe that will keep your business fully shod.

Once you have embraced the five daily disciplines, you need to utilize them by making measurable progress in generating leads each and every day—winning the day. The value of a single day is often lost when an individual feels overwhelmed. But each day you can win by taking a few small steps in the right direction.

The Win-the-Day Formula

Below is a formula that has helped many of our clients apply a Personal Business Standard and take action. Use this template as a guideline to customize your own Win-the-Day Formula. And what's most important is to have one. The Win-the-Day Formula keeps you accountable for your lead-generation activities each day of the year. Make sure you account for your lead-generation activities daily. As we all know, whatever gets measured, gets done.

> *Whatever gets measured, gets done.*

Daily

1. Write three personal notes.
2. Make five check-in calls.
3. Add one person to your database.

Weekly

1. Host two business lunches.
2. Average at least seven Pop-Bys.
3. Attend at least one networking meeting.

Monthly

1. Send an Item of Value to your entire database.
2. Make personal contact with all A+ clients.
3. Attend a business-networking event, such as those sponsored by the Chamber of Commerce, Business Network International (BNI) or LeTip International.

Quarterly

1. Host a networking party, seminar or gathering.
2. Update your business directory. (To learn more about creating a business directory, go to *www.takincareofbusiness.biz.*)

Yearly

1. Host a party for the people in your database.

Many times after I present at one of our Turning Point events, I'll spend time shaking hands and connecting with members of the audience. The most common question I'm asked is, "If the average Realtor only sells six homes annually, how are you able to sell more than 200 a year?" My answer is not sexy, but it is true: I have a set of meaningful goals, a proactive system of Working by Referral and disciplines I follow daily.

When you execute your daily disciplines, potential customers will become abundant. Now it's time to convert each and every potential customer into a patron of your business. In the next chapter, you will gain insight into giving Customer Service that will leave your competition in the dust.

Alber's Story:
Small Steps to Greatness

Growing up in Palestine, Alber Saleh fostered his entrepreneurial spirit by watching his father, Elias, operate a small jewelry business. Wanting more for his six children, however, Elias packed up his family and emigrated from Palestine to America in 1976, settling in San Francisco when Alber was just nine years old. The young boy witnessed his father find his way in a new culture and work many different odd jobs for long hours to put food on the table. Ultimately, Elias took a sales job at a Ford dealership and within a few short years, he was one of the top salespeople in the nation. Learning from his dad's work ethic and listening to his stories, Alber was inspired to take advantage of all the opportunities America offered.

To put himself through college, Alber worked as a bank teller. Bringing his entrepreneurial mindset to his job, he was promoted many times and ultimately was given the chance to build his own book of business.

Today he excels as a private mortgage banker for Wells Fargo where he was one of the first mortgage bankers to fund more than a billion dollars in loans. Alber's admitted secret to success is a complete focus on making every opportunity count. Unlike the typical mortgage banker who focuses primarily on the details of a transaction, he realizes there are many relationships inside a transaction that can be extremely beneficial. He builds relationships not just with clients but also with the attorneys, financial planners and accountants involved in each transaction—all of whom have the potential to be sources of new customers in the months and years ahead. How does Alber build and nurture these relationships? He maintains a Personal Business Standard that incorporates the daily disciplines of writing notes, making phone calls, and going to lunch and coffee with clients. These simple daily habits, executed consistently, have made him a legend in his industry, and they can do the same for you.

SECTION II

The Customer Experience

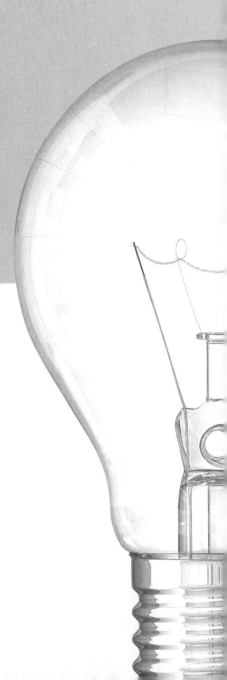

Takin' Care of
Customers

Brian Buffini

Not the maker of plans and promises, but rather the one who offers faithful service in small matters. This is the person who is most likely to achieve what is good and lasting.

– Johann Wolfgang von Goethe

CHAPTER SIX

Takin' Care of Customers

Brian Buffini

I t was 7 p.m. on December 23, 2007. My eight-year-old son, Adam, and I were half-walking, half-running through the mall. I'd been promising for weeks to take him to KB Toys, a national chain, so he could buy his siblings their Christmas gifts. His list even included pictures of the toys he wanted to buy, which he had downloaded for the shopping spree.

I worried that there would be slim pickings so close to Christmas, but I wasn't prepared for what we actually encountered. "Do you have any Star Wars Lego sets?" I asked the young clerk behind the counter. Without even a glance at us, she barked, "I don't know."

After searching the aisles on our own, we did find one of the Star Wars sets on Adam's list, but the box was opened and looked as though it was missing pieces. I approached a second salesperson who was walking the aisles to *assist customers*. When I asked whether there was another set in better condition, I received a curt response: "Whatever's on the floor is all we have."

As a business owner, I place a high value not only on serving my customers, but also on how I'm treated as a customer myself. Even though I held the hopes of an eight-year-old in my hands that evening, I couldn't settle for this type of service. I took Adam outside and said, "Son, I know we're under pressure for time, but there's an important lesson to learn here. We can never support a business or company that treats people like this." Fortunately Adam's disappointment was short-lived; we found another store that carried everything he wanted to buy.

I'll never forget the day, some years later, when Adam brought me a news story about KB Toys, with its hundreds of stores nationwide, going out of business. While it saddens me every time I hear of any business failing, I couldn't help wonder how much of a role poor Customer Service played in the company's demise. The way we treat our customers does have consequences.

Customer Disservice

The greatest value of excellent Customer Service is in making customers feel satisfied with the services, products and experiences they've purchased. Customers want to feel they are important and appreciated. Give them poor Customer Service, and they feel devalued. Remember that Customer Service is your job. It is required to build a solid business. Your Customer Service should be the gold standard by which other businesses gauge their own efforts.

> *The greatest value of excellent Customer Service is in making customers feel satisfied with the services, products and experiences they've purchased.*

In today's economy, where profit margins are slim and businesses are struggling to create demand in a stagnant market, companies have become very bottom-line focused. Watching the bottom line is never a bad thing, but some expenses can't be quantitatively measured. How do you measure the value of a satisfied customer, a job well done or continued good will?

Unfortunately, many companies have allowed their CFOs to define their Customer Service, and Customer Service is often seen as simply an expense to the business when examined on a profit and loss statement. As a result, Customer Service jobs have become low-paying jobs in many large organizations. Other companies have replaced people by using automated phone trees or e-mail to handle their Customer Service functions.

Now, I'm all for convenience and the use of technology, but doggone it, sometimes it's nice to talk to a real human being who can actually help you. It's exasperating when you're forced to hang up because your problem doesn't quite fit into any of the options the automated voice provides. Big and small companies alike must strike a healthy balance between automation and live Customer Service.

Buffini & Company uses automated phone trees, but we always let people know there's a live person waiting to talk to them. We use the Internet to handle frequently asked questions, but Customer Service representatives, whom we call our Client Care Team, are always available for a live conversation. Buffini & Company considers front-line employees, such as our receptionists, sales force, and Customer Service representatives, to be vital to the goodwill of our business. Receptionists, for example, have the title CFI, which is short for Creator of First Impressions. They are our customers' first contact at the company, and we want them to recognize the critical role they play. We also use recorded webinars and webcasts to provide information on products and training, but we couple them with live events and personal Coaching to create a customized experience for our clients.

Customer Disservice Can Cost You Big!

In October 2007, wildfires consumed our California home and everything we owned, including a matching pair of Mercedes in the driveway. All of our papers and records disappeared in the fire, and the insurance company needed the VIN numbers of both vehicles in order to send us a check to replace the cars. I called the dealership where I had purchased the cars and explained my situation in detail.

"Sir, I can't help you," was the reply. "I can't verify you are the owner of the automobile if I don't have the VIN number."

"I don't have the VIN numbers," I replied, "The cars are smoldering on my driveway, and the bill of sale burned up."

I patiently restated my need three different ways before asking to speak to the receptionist's supervisor. Her boss got on the phone and gave me the same answer, even though I offered to e-mail photos of the two charred auto carcasses on my driveway. He wouldn't budge. Obviously, this was a highly stressful time for me. The dealership was in the same geographic area as my home and had narrowly escaped the fire. Yet the two people I spoke to showed zero empathy or understanding for my situation. Their rigid responses communicated to me that they didn't care. Finally, out of sheer frustration, I asked the manager, "How clueless are you? I'm a guy with two burned up cars who will be getting an insurance settlement to buy two new ones."

> *Providing good old-fashioned Customer Service is the greatest niche small companies can fill in today's market.*

The insurance company finally came through and I bought two new cars, but not from that dealership. By simply showing some concern for my plight, the dealership could have had my business not just that day, but for life. Instead it became the subject of a cautionary tale on how to lose a customer.

It's Time to Turn Back the Clock

I believe that providing good old-fashioned Customer Service is the greatest niche small companies can fill in today's market. Treating customers well distinguishes your company from larger, more impersonal businesses. As larger companies consolidate and stores turn into megastores, small businesses can differentiate themselves by building more personal relationships with their customers.

An independent restaurant near Sea-Tac airport in Seattle, Washington, does a great job of providing exemplary Customer Service. Sharp's Roaster & Alehouse is 1,000 miles from my home, but I've eaten there numerous times when I've presented to audiences in Seattle. Over the years, a waiter at the restaurant, Tony, and I have connected to the degree that he knows not only my name, but what I like to eat and drink for lunch!

> *As larger companies consolidate and stores turn into megastores, small businesses can differentiate themselves by building more personal relationships with their customers.*

Recently I took my son, AJ, on a road trip with me to a Turning Point event in Seattle. I had not been to Sharp's for a while, so I took the opportunity to visit. As soon as we walked in the door, Tony approached with a couple of menus, showed us to our table, and asked, "Well, Mr. Buffini, do you still drink Arnold Palmers and enjoy a chicken teriyaki bowl?"

Now that's not just good old-fashioned Customer Service; that's the way to make an advocate. We were in Seattle for four days, and I took 20 of my staff members to eat at Sharp's three times! I also announced to 2,000 locals who were attending our event that Sharp's was a great restaurant with superb Customer Service.

In 1936, Dale Carnegie wrote the timeless book, "How to Win Friends and Influence People." This book should be mandatory reading for all small-business owners. Carnegie's principles for winning friends and influencing people are exactly the same guidelines for winning customers and building advocates. At Buffini & Company, we've boiled down Carnegie's principles (and added a few of our own) into eight essential rules for providing exemplary Customer Service.

1. Exude Positive Energy

You've probably heard it said that 75 percent of our communication is nonverbal. Consider how people respond to someone else's energy—or lack of it. When you see someone yawn, chances are you'll be yawning yourself seconds later. Or, have you ever felt a jolt of energy when a store clerk or hotel employee flashes you a great smile? When you and your employees exude positive energy, your customers will not only reflect it back but will form a favorable impression of you and your company.

2. Look People in the Eye

The simple act of looking your customers in the eyes communicates a powerful nonverbal message. It says: *I value you, you're a priority* and *you have my full attention.* Eye contact also conveys trust and sincerity. If you want to succeed in business, looking someone in the eye is the first step to building trusting, sincere relationships with your customers.

3. Use the Magic Words

All parents share the same goal of wanting to instill basic manners in their children. I can't count the number of times I told my own kids, "Courtesy and respect cost you nothing, but they are worth everything." And if that didn't have the desired effect, I'd resort to quoting Bill Cosby: "You know, I brought you in this world, and I can take you out. And it don't make no difference to me, I'll make another one look just like you." Something must have clicked with my kids because when we're at a restaurant as a family, waitresses frequently remark, "Your kids are so polite and well-mannered. It's so refreshing to see." All this because my children will say, "Can I have macaroni and cheese, please?" And when it's delivered, they say, "Thank you."

If you've ever done business with someone who didn't even look up to say, "Thank you," then you know how dehumanized that lack of courtesy made you feel. When you and your staff treat customers with courtesy and respect, you'll be able to count on those customers returning—and referring others to your business.

4. Be an Attentive Listener

The most common complaint of dissatisfied customers is that they didn't feel heard. What the customer really means is that this business didn't understand his or her needs. Attentive listeners are aware of what's spoken and unspoken. In Stephen Covey's bestseller, "The Seven Habits of Highly Successful People," he advises, "Seek first to understand, then be understood." Naturally, we want customers to understand what we're offering, what we're selling and what the value is. But addressing our agenda before we understand our customers' needs says we're more interested in their money than we are in them.

> *Focusing on the transaction instead of your customers' needs is a short-term approach to sales that does not produce a long-standing business with profits.*

Focusing on the transaction instead of your customers' needs is a short-term approach to sales that does not produce a long-standing business with profits. Nor does it make a genuine connection with your customers, which is just as important as making a profit. I have many great memories of handing a young couple the keys to their first home. In some cases, those relationships are still strong today even though the money I earned from those transactions was spent long ago. Being an attentive listener creates an environment for you to have many rewarding customer experiences.

5. Remember Your Customers' Names

Dale Carnegie's most indelible piece of advice is that a person's name is, to that individual, the sweetest and most important word in any language. Don't take liberties with a person's name or be afraid to use Mr., Mrs. or Ms. with their last names. Ask how they'd like to be addressed. This practice may sound old-fashioned, but it demonstrates the respect you have for your customers.

> *If you want to be a profit-maker, you've got to be a promise-keeper.*

6. Don't Make Promises You Can't Keep

If you want to be a profit-maker, you've got to be a promise-keeper. Following through on promises, commitments and details is essential to building customer trust and loyalty. "Under-promise and over-deliver" is how the business adage goes, but I'd further refine it to, "Clearly communicate your promises and overly communicate your delivery." The most professional people I've encountered speak to me respectfully and clearly communicate all the details of how their product will be delivered or their service administered.

7. Pay Attention to What's Important to Your Customer

> *Noting what's important to your customer can often cement a business relationship.*

We've all had the experience of walking into a restaurant or store and being pleased that the waiter remembered our favorite beverage or a salesperson knew our preferences. Noting what's important to your customer can often cement a business relationship. Once your customers know you really care, your business becomes special enough for them to share it with their friends. No matter how small the detail, any observation and recollection of your customers' preferences transforms a transaction into a memorable personalized experience. At Buffini & Company, all of our Business Coaches are taught to treat an individual as if he or she is the only client the Coach has. And that's exactly how you want each of your clients to feel.

8. Don't Neglect the Follow-Up

Call, send a note or write an e-mail message to your customers after you've completed a transaction with them. The reason can be specific, such as to provide an answer to a question you said you'd research, or it can be to reiterate a promise you made, or simply to check if your customer has any further questions. Follow-up communication lets your customers know you're interested in them and not just their patronage, and it creates confidence in your company.

Turning back the clock to deliver good old-fashioned Customer Service can turn any business around. When you take care of your customers, your customers will take care of you by doing business with you again and again and ultimately referring their friends and family to you. A personal endorsement is the most powerful and least expensive way to generate new business, and your goal should be to turn every customer into an advocate. As the spokesman for Buffini & Company, I receive much of the praise and acknowledgement for the work the entire company does. I certainly play a role in the company's success, but many of the positive comments from clients are a direct result of the great experiences they've had with the staff of our company.

> *A personal endorsement is the most powerful and least expensive way to generate new business.*

Why Customers
Refer

Joe Niego

*Always try to maintain complete tolerance,
and always make an effort to give people more
than they expect.*

– Scott Hamilton

Why Customers Refer

Joe Niego

Recently Brian and I were speaking at an intimate gathering of highly successful business owners in picturesque Dana Point, California. During the lunch break, we decided to drive into town to get a bite to eat. We made the rookie mistake, however, of not asking the concierge at our hotel for a referral to a restaurant. And, as men are apt to do, we got in the car and started driving without any directions.

We were looking for a full-service restaurant since neither Brian nor I are into fast food. We pulled into the parking lot of one restaurant, but one quick glance through the windows told us the place was completely empty. That was not a good sign, so we drove a little further down the street until we spotted a line of people waiting to get into the Bonjour Café. We joined them and happily discovered that our dining experience was well worth the wait.

So why is it that two restaurants located just a block apart, offering the same cuisine, are experiencing two different levels of success: one thriving and one barely surviving? Though there are probably many reasons why one restaurant has a 45-minute wait to be seated and the other is vacant, the bottom line is customers will go where they see value. In this chapter, we'll reveal the three experiences that every customer could have and the one experience that keeps customers not only coming back but referring your business to others.

Expectations: The Bedrock of Customer Experience

Having owned a real estate company for more than 24 years that has sold more than 2,500 homes, I've had my share of customer interactions. In my years of research on why consumers make the choices they do, I've found that everyone has a pre-existing frame of reference (expectation) for what a particular business encounter *should* look like. Usually, customers have had a similar experience to draw from, have spoken with someone they trust about their experiences or have developed expectations through their own research. For example, if you're planning to dine at a particular restaurant, you might have a certain expectation based on a previous meal you had there, a friend's dining experience or a newspaper review. Past experience leads to future expectations. Similarly, an expectation may be formed by a promise you were given, such as when your accountant states that he'll have your tax return finished by the end of the week!

> *The ultimate goal of your business should be to always exceed what your customers expect.*

Regardless of how an individual's expectation is first created, if you violate that expectation you can expect conflict and unhappy customers. Falling below customers' expectations guarantees they won't use your services again and definitely won't refer you to others.

But customers who receive more value than they anticipated *want* to share you with the people they care about because it makes them feel good to do so. The ultimate goal of your business should be to always exceed what your customers expect. And the degree of your customers' loyalty and desire to refer others to you is directly related to how much you exceed expectations.

The Referability Index

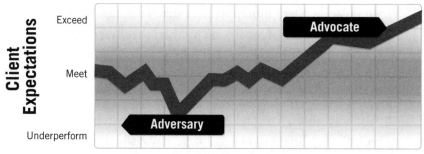

Client Experience

What the above Referability Index shows is that every time you underperform in a client's eyes, he or she takes one step closer to becoming an adversary. But every small step you take to exceed your customers' expectations brings them closer to being advocates for you and your company. You've heard it said that, "A happy client may tell two or three people, but an unhappy client will tell the world." And in today's highly connected world of social networking and online communities, clients literally *can* share with the world their negative impressions of your company.

Three Customer Experiences

I want to share with you three customer experiences with photographers that bring the Referability Index to life. One experience created adversarial customers, one was a neutral experience involving a fair exchange of photography services for the price paid, and the last was an exceptional experience that turned customers into advocates.

The degree of your customers' loyalty and desire to refer others to you is directly related to how much you exceed expectations.

1. Making an Adversary

When customers are unhappy, it's usually because they've received something of lesser quality than they were expecting. If your services and products fall below your customers' expectations, you'll lose not only customers but also potential referrals.

My wife, Julie, has a real passion for photography. Since she was a little girl, she and her dad have always had a special bond that revolved around their mutual love of photos. So you can imagine how important it was to Julie that our wedding photos be terrific. On our wedding day, Julie was very attuned to what the photographer was doing. The problem was, he wasn't attuned to her!

By nature Julie is very gracious and easygoing. But I watched her anxiety build throughout the day as the photographer missed one after another of the candid photos we had requested. When he took the formal photos, he seemed content to settle for the first shot rather than taking multiple pictures to capture the moment in the best possible way.

Two months later, when we sat with the photographer to view our wedding album, Julie could not hide her disappointment. Julie normally never has a bad word to say about anyone—with one exception! Over the years many of our family members and friends have heard her say, "Whatever you do, don't use our wedding photographer."

2. The Fair Exchange

Companies that manage to stay in business obviously don't have a large number of adversarial clients. But what many businesses settle for is the *Fair Exchange*, i.e., they deliver exactly what they promise for the price the customer is quoted. That's the experience we had with the second photographer.

We're always adding to our collection of photos of our kids, parents, grandparents and extended family that grace the walls of our home. When we wanted a photo of our entire extended family, Julie juggled everybody's schedules and managed to get us all to a local photography studio on a Saturday morning. The photographer organized us in rows in front of a plain background and began shooting. But when we tried to strike various poses and suggest different arrangements, we were told our time was up.

When we left the studio, I asked Julie for her thoughts about the shoot. She was decidedly neutral. As promised, we received the 10 photos, but nowhere among them were the two or three memorable shots that would have wowed us. Would we use this studio again? Perhaps, but only if we couldn't find a better option. Truthfully, I've forgotten the name of it, which pretty much guarantees I won't be recommending it to others.

Interestingly, many business owners believe that if you give customers what they pay for, they will be satisfied and automatically come back. After all, the customer's needs were fulfilled, and basic expectations were met. And those business owners are right; some of these satisfied customers will return if it's convenient for them to do so.

But will these customers refer your business to others? Not likely. Satisfied clients rarely refer. In order for your customers to proactively advocate for your product or services, they must be impressed, feel special, get a little something extra they weren't expecting or feel that doing business with you is highly convenient for them.

3. The Exceptional Experience

Customers who have had an exemplary experience with a business are usually bursting to tell others about it. My sister, Terry, for example, couldn't wait to tell Julie and me about Amy Tripple Photography (*www.amytripplephotography.com*). "This gal doesn't just take your photos; she captures your life experiences," Terry said, delighted with the photos Amy took of her family.

Terry was so adamant about the extraordinary quality of

> *Customers who have had an exemplary experience with a business are usually bursting to tell others about it.*

Amy's work that we called the studio that same day. But instead of providing details about her charges and availability, the photographer started interviewing us. She wanted to know our boys' names, ages, hobbies and interests. She asked questions about our lifestyle and the types of photos we'd be interested in seeing. When Julie and I hung up the phone, we had a great sense of excitement about the upcoming appointment and felt we hadn't just met a photographer, but a new friend. Based on our previous encounters with photographers, this initial contact with Amy far exceeded our expectations.

We chose a local forest preserve for the photo shoot, which I thought would take hours. It didn't. Within 45 minutes, Amy had captured the essence of our kids' personalities. During the photo shoot, Amy even offered tips to Julie on how to use our own camera to get more from our photos. And, as Terry had promised, we couldn't have been happier with the photos we received.

Even after receiving our final photos from the session, Amy continued to exceed our expectations. We began receiving a monthly e-mail from Amy's studio that continued to cement our relationship. Similar to the eReport discussed in Chapter Four, Amy sent tips such as, "How to properly frame a picture," "How to build a collage" and "Ten things you need to know about a camera." She also included online resources for accessing and storing photos and videos, links to great photography websites and a look at her photography portfolio.

If you give your clients an extraordinary experience, not only will they loyally return to your business time after time, but they'll also tell others about you.

Nine months after our first photo shoot, I called Amy to do another. Word had definitely spread that Amy continually goes the extra mile; her calendar was booked months in advance. When her assistant scheduled our appointment into Amy's heavily booked calendar, she told me that Amy would be looking forward to taking photos of my family—a comment that made me feel valued. As you can tell, I've become an advocate for Amy Tripple Photography. She doesn't just do a great job taking photos; she gives the type of Customer Service that builds her business. Today, many members of our large extended family are Amy's customers because I've referred them to her.

Remember, Sales & Marketing is the most important leg of your stool. If you give your clients an extraordinary experience, not only will they loyally return to your business time after time, but they'll also tell others about you.

In the next chapter, we'll share tips, ideas and strategies for adding value to the services you offer. We call them The Unexpected Extras, and they will create fiercely loyal customers as well as a continuous stream of referrals to your business.

Doing The
Unexpected
Extras

Joe Niego

It's never crowded along the extra mile.

– Wayne Dyer

Doing The Unexpected Extras

Joe Niego

My father, Ron Niego, owned Meta Concrete, a one-truck cement company that poured hundreds of miles of sidewalks and driveways throughout Chicago's south side. During our summer breaks from high school, my four brothers and I worked alongside him in the business. My dad's small business supported our family, but he also used it as a tool to teach his boys some very valuable lessons.

When we arrived at a job site, we would tear out the old sidewalk and pour the new concrete. That would be the end of the job for most cement companies. But my dad didn't work that way. As the concrete was drying, we'd take out a wire brush and walk around the job site looking for any stains that might have been left behind. We'd scrub and remove those stains, whether or not we were responsible for them. Then we'd rake the grass for any errant stones that might get caught in the homeowner's lawnmower. After we stripped the cement forms, we'd fill the void with black dirt instead of leaving the typical gap that's common in the masonry trade. Grass that we cut out was replaced and watered as if it had never been disturbed. "Leave it better than you found it, boys," was my dad's refrain.

While we were completing the final touches, my dad would assess our work. Only when it met his standard did he impress *Meta Concrete* and our home phone number into the still-wet concrete with a brass stamp.

Today, when I visit the south side of Chicago, I still see many of the sidewalks and driveways with *Meta Concrete* permanently embedded in them. My dad wasn't just trying to make an impression on the concrete; he was trying to make an impression on his clients. He never set out to simply satisfy clients. It was important to him to always exceed clients' expectations, and it paid off in the waiting list of people who wanted Meta Concrete to do work for them.

This chapter will define The Unexpected Extras concept and provide some ideas on how to implement this in your business. The Unexpected Extras are to your business what mints on a pillow are to the hotel business. It's often the small gesture that pays the biggest dividends in your business. For example, after my car dealership has serviced my vehicle, they deliver it to me with the interior vacuumed and the exterior washed. I could take my car to several drive-thru service stations that would be more convenient for me. But I choose

> *It's often the small gesture that pays the biggest dividends in your business.*

to drive a greater distance to the dealership because of the little extras they do. How much does it cost to wash a car? Not that much. But the time it saves me in not having to get my car washed that week and the care it communicates are, as the commercial says, "priceless."

Just as my father built his customer base by doing The Unexpected Extras, you can also create advocates for your business by enhancing your customers' interactions with your company. But first you have to know what your customers value most. If you're not sure, get in the habit of speaking with your clients regularly and asking them for their input. For example, a great thing to ask your best customers, especially those who endorse you to others, is, "I'm just curious what you tell people when you refer them to my business." They won't just mention the core service you provide; they'll tell you about some of the smaller things that, to them, were The Unexpected Extras.

Here are five different ways to apply The Unexpected Extras in your business, which you can tailor to your customers' needs and your industry.

1. Go Above and Beyond

In every customer interaction, there is a required level of performance. But going above and beyond, time and time again, is a phenomenal way to ensure customer loyalty and referrals. Cortney Gill is an excellent example of someone who embodies The Unexpected Extras. Her swelling client base is evidence that it works.

Cortney Gill was running a property management business with just 20 customers in San Antonio, Texas, when she first heard of our Working by Referral system. Just a few short years later, her monthly income has skyrocketed from $1,200 to $12,000 and she has a portfolio of 129 properties.

Cortney goes above and beyond her customers' expectations, and they know it. Typically, a property owner hears from a manager only when there's a problem. Cortney's customers hear from her every month. "We do property drive-bys, interior inspections with pictures and a report that grades the home and offers suggestions on how to improve it," says Cortney. She also sends customers updates on local markets and quarterly landlord-related financial tips from her CPA. And when the properties need repairs, Cortney taps her network of quality tradespeople with whom she's negotiated discounts. "I also call my customers monthly simply to check in, I write them personal notes and I send them a little gift quarterly, no matter where they are in the country," said Cortney. "My customers can go to sleep at night with peace of mind that their properties are in good hands."

Cortney's recent business success has had a radical impact on her personal life. A single mom, Cortney has managed to pay off $102,000 in credit card debt, buy her own home and invest in real estate. Recently her young brother was diagnosed with brain cancer, and her savings and sound investments have allowed her to help pay medical bills and support her parents while they care for their son.

"This is not my job but my passion," Cortney said. "I am constantly looking for ways to go above and beyond what my customers expect. And, because of that, my business has done well and the quality of my life is much better than I had hoped for."

2. Give Something Extra

An excellent way to reinforce a buying decision your customer just made is to throw in a small product or service without cost. Everyone loves receiving something for free, and it's an investment that will pay dividends for you in the long run.

> *An excellent way to reinforce a buying decision your customer just made is to throw in a small product or service without cost.*

Over the last five years, a good friend of mine has been trying to talk me into buying a road bike so I can join his biking group. After I exhausted every possible excuse, I finally relented and said I'd buy a road bike. "Go see Mark at The Wheel Thing," said my friend. "He'll take good care of you."

Mark spent an hour and a half helping me choose the right model and get the proper fit. He also recommended bike routes, taught me the biking rules of the road and gave me some maintenance tips. After talking about the importance of keeping my tires inflated at the proper pressure, we realized I didn't have the right kind of air pump. Mark grabbed one from behind the counter and gave it to me, waving off my attempt to pay for it. "The pump's on me," he said. This simple gesture made me feel he valued me more than my money. Since then, I've purchased bikes for my children and a road bike for Julie, all from Mark.

3. Notice a Need

While you're interacting with your customers, take time to determine if they have an immediate need or challenge that you might help them address. Fixing a problem they're having may turn out to be The Unexpected Extra that makes their day.

Ray Johnson is the owner of Iron Fitness Extremes (*www.ironfitnessextremes.com*) where Julie and I both work out. Ray trains us with kettle bells (weighted balls with handles on them) to help us gain strength, create flexibility and build endurance. The main reason I enjoy working out with Ray is because of his knowledge and passion for his work. He excels at finding ways to do The Unexpected Extras for his customers.

For example, when Julie was doing a swinging motion that caused the weight to repeatedly bump against her forearm, Ray made a mental note of it. When we arrived at our next workout, he had two sets of padded sweatbands ready so both of us could protect our forearms. Ray took the time not just to notice a need, but also to fill it—without prompting. I've since referred Iron Fitness Extreme to members of my family and I've featured Ray at seminars in our hometown of Chicago.

4. Make it Right, Then Make it Better

No doubt you've had the experience of returning a faulty product to a store. Sometimes you were offered an apology or a manager gave you a refund or exchanged the item for another in working order. You probably thought the store handled the situation correctly. Well, not necessarily. If you're trying to build a business and create advocates, the best way to handle a problem is to leave the customer better off than they were before the transaction.

> *If you're trying to build a business and create advocates, the best way to handle a problem is to leave the customer better off than they were before the transaction.*

For our 15-year wedding anniversary, Julie and I went to a steakhouse where I ordered a filet mignon cooked medium-well. What I received was a rare steak, which I sent back to the kitchen to be cooked exactly to order. The restaurant had corrected its error to my satisfaction, but at the conclusion of the meal, the server brought us two pieces of New York cheesecake for dessert and two cups of coffee on the house.

The restaurant didn't stop when it made my steak right. Instead, it made my dining experience better than I had expected with a complimentary course. Now every time we have a special occasion in our family, we celebrate it at this wonderful restaurant. The complimentary dessert and coffee was a great investment on the part of the restaurant—and of course I've more than compensated the restaurant for the price of The Unexpected Extras since then.

5. Take a Personal Interest

In today's fast-paced world, consumers often feel that the companies they do business with treat them more like numbers than individuals. But when customers feel as if you are taking the time and interest to personally get to know them, they often become your customers for life.

My oldest sister, Mary McNamara, owns a small business just like I do. As an attorney, she focuses on real estate closings, wills, probate and trusts. Many of her clients have never engaged the services of an attorney before. Therefore, when they meet Mary for the first time, they are nervous and a little uptight. In no time, however, Mary makes her clients feel at ease because of the personal interest she takes in them. One widow needed a 10-minute adjustment to her will, which stretched into an hour-and-a-half appointment because the woman was nervous and alone. Mary

> *When customers feel as if you are taking the time and interest to personally get to know them, they often become your customers for life.*

gave her client all her attention and never charged her for the extended visit. Because Mary demonstrates in numerous ways that she has her clients' best interests at heart, she never has to advertise or promote herself. Her business has a constant stream of incoming referrals from people she has served in the past.

Unexpected Extras for You

Here are a few other ways that business owners have incorporated Unexpected Extras into their products and services.

House painter Rodrigo Evangelista buys new socks for his painting team each time they start a new job. Rodrigo figured that customers would appreciate knowing that the painters who were taking off their shoes to work inside the house were wearing new socks. And Rodrigo was right.

....

Home inspector/owner of Inspect-It 1st in Arizona, Marty Lenich goes the extra mile with his clients by personally meeting with them to present his findings and recommendations on the houses they hope to buy or sell. In face-to-face meetings, clients freely ask him questions, which takes away some of the stress and worry of buying or selling a house. Grateful clients thank their Realtors for introducing them to Marty, and these Realtors, in turn, refer their customers and fellow agents to Marty.

....

Allen and Meredith Warren own Jones Warren Construction, a company that specializes in insurance claim services and is recognized as the number-one reclamation company in Birmingham, Alabama. Recently, the Warrens' company remodeled a large office for one of their A+ customers. What did the Warrens do that was so special? They did all the work after hours and on weekends so there was no disruption to the client's business—while charging normal rates and insisting that the subcontractors do the same.

In another case, the Warrens spent five hours securing a home immediately after a fire damaged it last Halloween. "The family was so concerned about being looted that we had our framers build a temporary wall that night," said Allen. As a result of their diligence, the home was secure and so was their relationship with the client.

....

Mary Vierthaler is a Realtor in Tucson, Arizona, one of the hardest-hit housing markets in the United States. Mary has continued to prosper despite the downturn because she knows her clients and caters to them, inviting them to parties and sending them small gifts. When she discovered that one of her A+ clients liked hiking, she found a trail, arranged the hike and even went along.

....

Deann Blausey's court-reporting agency in Santa Rosa, California is known for the extraordinary service it provides. "In the morning I serve my attorney clients fresh-ground coffee, orange juice, fresh pastries, fruit, yogurt, biscotti and energy bars," explains Deann. "In the afternoon I bring out the See's candy, fresh-baked cookies, sodas, sparkling water and fruit." A client who needs lunch will get an offer from Deann to pick up a sandwich at the local Italian deli. She's happy to send a car to the airport to pick up a client who has just flown in. The trial starts tomorrow and the client needs another transcript? Deann sends it immediately—at no additional charge. By being the go-to person, Deann has fostered the loyalty of a large group of attorneys and easily recoups costs of these Unexpected Extras with the volume of business she gets in return.

Do The Unexpected Extras for your customers and you may receive an unexpected extra profit each and every year. And in the following two chapters, you'll acquire step-by-step strategies on how to handle the money you make.

SECTION III

Financial Management

CHAPTER NINE

Staying in
Sequence

Brian Buffini

*We delight in the beauty of the butterfly, but
rarely admit the changes it has gone through
to achieve that beauty.*

– Maya Angelou

Staying in Sequence

Brian Buffini

T here's an old Italian proverb that says, "One hand washes the other, both hands wash the face." I like to use this proverb to illustrate how intertwined your personal and business finances are. Think of your one hand as your personal finances and the other hand as your business finances. When your personal finances and your business finances work in harmony, you have peace of mind in your personal life and in your business. For many small businesses, the lines between personal and professional finances are often blurred. I've often heard it said that you're not really an entrepreneur until you've had to write a personal check to cover payroll.

I've certainly experienced times in my career when I've had to sacrifice personal assets to support a business in a season it wasn't profitable. The area of personal finances can be a source of overwhelming stress and can cause strife in personal relationships. Business owners will take the time to pay their bills, but they often don't allocate any time to create a financial strategy or plan for their company.

The most tangible success we've seen at Buffini & Company is the transformation in the lives of our clients as their personal and professional finances come under control. It's inspiring when you see a financially stressed individual become empowered because a former area of weakness is now an area of strength. I cannot give enough credit to our incredible Coaches who facilitate this change in clients on a daily basis.

In this chapter, you'll learn the principle of Sequence to achieve stability in your personal finances. I'll also share a series of action steps that have produced great results for many people.

A word of caution, however: the principles and steps laid out for you in this chapter take time. Remember the punch line to the question, "How do you eat an elephant?" "One bite at a time!" And that's how you must view your finances. With each step you take and every check mark you place next to one of our action steps, take heart that you are making progress and are on the right path.

The Concept of Sequence

The concept of Sequence is one of the most important lessons I've learned about money. Everyday life is filled with sequences, or events that move in a chronological and logical order. A child gains mobility by progressing from crawling to walking to running. Students move through the educational system by attending first preschool, then elementary school, middle school, high school, and possibly college and graduate school. In a romantic sequence, couples advance from courtship to engagement to marriage.

The sequence of financial prosperity also follows a natural progression: Survival, Stability, Success and Significance. This sequence was first identified by the renowned Zig Ziglar—mentor and close friend to Joe and me—who uses it as the basis for his self-help programs. Not everyone will start at the same stage in the sequence. Those who have extreme debt and are spending beyond their means will have to progress through more stages than individuals who are paying their bills, but not saving enough for retirement.

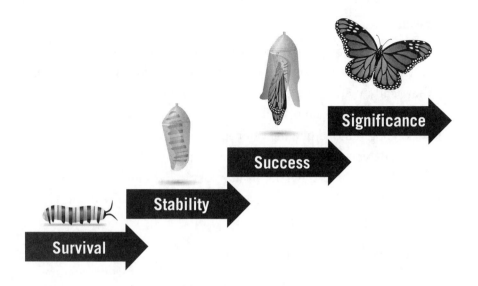

The financial sequence can be likened to the metamorphosis of a caterpillar into a Monarch butterfly. In order for a caterpillar to undergo its transformation, it must follow precise steps in a defined order. You'll never see a caterpillar grow wings overnight; nature remains true to its design and there is no hurrying the process. The struggle that ensues in the darkness of the cocoon is also vital to the metamorphosis. Before a butterfly can achieve the ultimate freedom of flight, it must fight to release itself from the confinement of its chrysalis.

Each stage of your own financial sequence has a purpose and importance, and none can be hurried or done out of order.

Each stage of your own financial sequence has a purpose and importance, and none can be hurried or done out of order. And while it won't be easy to change ingrained spending habits, with discipline and incremental steps you can sever the monetary bonds that have constrained you from reaching your financial potential. Let's take a look at the characteristics of each phase and the steps necessary to move from Survival to Significance.

Survival

When you are in Survival mode, you feel like you've reached rock bottom. Your expenses and debt are crushing, and your current income is drastically inadequate to meet your financial obligations. Bills go unpaid, credit cards are maxed out, and savings are nonexistent. Right now you're grounded like the caterpillar.

Perhaps you feel your situation is helpless because you don't see how you'll be able to crawl out from under the weight of your financial burdens. The good news is there's nowhere to go but up—provided you start taking steps in the right direction.

1. Incrementally Increase Your Income

The biggest mistake entrepreneurs make when their finances are in crisis is to chase some radical idea that promises to return a huge amount of money in a short amount of time. Now, it's not that this scenario can't happen; it's just that the most significant success follows an incremental path of growth. Imagine a professional baseball player trying to make a major league team. The difference between playing at a major league level or in the minors is the difference between making millions or making thousands. A common mistake among rookie players is to try to hit a home run every time. In truth, what that young man needs to do is to focus on getting one hit. A baseball player who hits .250 is at risk of losing his job, but a player who hits .300 is a superstar. The difference is five extra hits every 100 times at bat.

If you focus on the Big Idea for Small Business and the practical strategies we suggest in this book, you can increase your average income and become a superstar, too.

2. Keep Your Cash Liquid

My dad used to say, "When you're on top of the mountain, throw a little dirt in the valley; it'll break your fall." The dirt in the valley is an amount of cash you keep in reserve that you can access at all times. Start your emergency fund with $1,000, and keep contributing to it until you've built a cash cushion that will cover your home expenses for one month. Then build the fund to cover three months of expenses, then six months. You'll be well on your way to the next level—Stability.

3. Institute a Spending Freeze at Home

A common mistake people make when trying to right their financial ship is to remove one or two major items from their budget. Although plenty of individuals' personal finances have recently collapsed under the weight of mortgages they couldn't afford, frequently it's the cumulative effect of smaller, unmonitored expenditures that break budgets. I'm talking about paying $5 for a cup of coffee 10 times a week instead of brewing your own, not preparing meals so you're forced to eat out, buying subscriptions to magazines and services that are just not necessary and going to the grocery store without a list so you wind up with a cart full of impulse purchases. There is a big difference between essential needs (food) and wants (premium cable). Carefully review your monthly expenses, and eliminate any that are not necessary for your basic needs.

> *Using cash heightens your awareness of what you are spending.*

4. Pay with Cash

Using cash heightens your awareness of what you are spending. Las Vegas casinos, for example, use poker chips as a stand-in for cash to get people to forget they're betting real money. Another benefit to carrying only cash is that when your cash is gone, it's gone. You can't spend money you don't have.

I typically allow myself a certain amount of cash each month for incidental spending. It's become a game with me to see if I can get by on the same amount of monthly cash I allocated to myself years ago. I can and I do! For further cash strategies, go to *www.daveramsey.com* and look into his *envelope system*.

5. Get Your Family on the Same Page

A house divided against itself cannot stand. If you share your life with someone, it's important that you try to get on the same page economically. Having been married for more than 20 years, I encourage couples to at least try to get on the same chapter if staying on the same page is impossible. Failing that, try the same book! The key is to focus on your common financial goals rather than areas of contention. Begin with what you both value, and let the list grow over the years.

Stability

You can claim financial stability when your income stream is predictable, you're paying your monthly bills on time and you're not acquiring any additional debt, i.e., you're living within your means. Congratulate yourself for making great strides and addressing your most pressing financial challenges. Now let's look at some steps to fortify your financial foundation.

> *A home without a budget is like a car without brakes.*

1. Establish a Home Budget

A home without a budget is like a car without brakes. What is going to stop you from living beyond your means? How do you harness your emotional impulses to purchase? Establish a budget and stick to it. Record the amounts you typically spend in all the major home categories. Go to *www.takincareofbusiness.biz*, download a copy of the sample budget and use it as a framework to establish your baseline expenses. This will take you less than 45 minutes, but it is the most powerful tool we know of for changing impulse purchases into informed decisions.

2. Set up an Automatic Transfer into a Savings Account

It's critical that you develop a monthly savings habit. Initially, the amount doesn't matter as much as the action of putting money away. Start small and you can increase the amount over time.

I recommend you go to your bank and set up an automatic withdrawal from your checking into your savings account. (I make transfers on the 3rd and 17th of each month.) You probably already have payments that are automatically withdrawn from

> *Debt reduction takes time and requires a plan.*

your account each month. Consider monthly deposits into your savings account a non-negotiable payment. We've all heard the expression, "Pay yourself first." With this strategy, you're doing exactly that. As your business prospers, increase the amount you transfer each month, and you'll be well on your way to financial success.

3. Develop a Debt-Reduction Plan

You didn't get into debt overnight, so don't expect to get out of debt immediately. Debt reduction takes time and requires a plan. Contact your debtors and construct a realistic payment plan. Our Business Coaches developed a program we call the Rollover Plan, and helping people become debt-free is one of the joys of their job. Go to *www.takincareofbusiness.biz* for a detailed outline of the Rollover Plan. There are many strategies to reduce debt, but this is the one we've found that works best for small-business owners.

4. Be Properly Insured

Insurance premiums are among the most difficult payments to make. You shell out money at regular intervals for protection you hope you and your family won't have to use. But without the safety net of insurance, a serious illness, disability or your death can mean financial ruin for you and your heirs. Financial stability requires that you have sufficient medical, life and disability insurance. Get a referral from someone you trust to a financial planner or insurance broker. But don't just buy insurance. Develop an insurance plan that protects you and your loved ones for the short-, mid- and long-term.

5. Have a Written Will

According to *www.findlaw.com,* 58 percent of American adults do not have a written will, which means they are relinquishing control over how their assets will be distributed after they die and who will become the guardians of their minor children. A will is a basic component of estate planning. Without a will, the laws of the state and the decisions of a probate court may determine how your estate is distributed and who will care for your children if they are minors.

Once you've checked off all the boxes under Stability, you may be feeling pretty good about yourself. But ambitious entrepreneurs often aspire to attain the next phase of the Sequence—Success.

Success

You may think you're living on easy street when your income far exceeds your expenses, your savings account is flush, all consumer debt is paid off and you have disposable income. But newly acquired financial gains can also make you passive and cause you to take your foot off the gas. Remember, the Big Idea for Small Business is that Sales &

Marketing is what ultimately drive your business. When some people reach financial stability, they tend to pull back on marketing, which is the fuel necessary to drive further business success.

Here are five tips to help you reach financial success:

1. Invest in Yourself

Benjamin Franklin is widely considered to be America's first millionaire. He had one dominant investment strategy: "If a man empties his purse into his head, no man can take it away from him. An investment in knowledge always pays the best interest." A small business will only grow as far as the owner grows. One of my mentors, the great Jim Rohn, told me that if I worked harder on myself than I did on my business, I'd make a fortune rather than just a living. He was right. Over the years I've been amply rewarded from the investments I've made in self-development books, tapes, CDs, seminars and coaching as my businesses have benefited from my personal growth.

> *A small business will only grow as far as the owner grows.*

2. Put Your Money to Work

When you follow the Sales & Marketing advice in this book, you generate more customer leads. With more leads, you make more sales. With more sales, you make more income. By following our budgeting advice, you create a financial surplus, which allows you to invest. Most small-business owners will pour excess funds into their own business. Putting all your eggs in one basket is dangerous, however. So invest in stocks, bonds and real estate. Neither Joe nor I are experts in investing, but we have both followed the principles of the world's greatest investor, Warren

Buffet, who advises investing only in what you know. If you don't fully understand it, don't buy it! If that's good enough for Warren Buffet, it's good enough for me.

3. Pay Off Your Home

There are many different opinions on this subject. Some people believe paying off a mortgage is a priority. Others believe it's wise to carry a mortgage, and, in many places, there are tax benefits for doing so. I personally believe that you should buy a home with an adequate down payment, secure a fixed-rate mortgage and then begin to make investments outside of your business.

I do encourage people to make additional principal payments to shorten the life of their home loans. But never agree to use your home as collateral for a business loan. No matter how well your business is doing, business cycles can abruptly change. It's challenging enough to endure a business crisis without worrying that a downturn will take away the roof over your family's head.

4. Develop a Detailed Retirement Plan

According to a recent Harris Interactive poll, 34 percent of Americans have not saved for retirement and 27 percent have no savings at all. Don't be a statistic. Get a referral from someone you trust to a financial advisor who takes a relational, long-term approach to advising his or her customers, and start planning for your retirement years. As my friend Zig Ziglar always says, "Failing to plan is planning to fail."

Significance

Significance is the last stage of your financial journey. You've finally broken free of financial limitations and are flying high. Financial worry is a distant memory now that you've achieved financial security and freedom. For many people, this is also the time to prepare their financial legacy.

Here are some tips:

1. Have a Plan

Create a plan to sell your business or develop a succession strategy for your heirs to take over your business after you retire or pass away.

2. Review Your Portfolio

Reallocate your investment portfolio from growth investments to those that will provide a steady stream of income so you can maintain your lifestyle without working.

3. Be Intentional with Your Financial Legacy

Whether you're planning to leave money or assets to children or grandchildren, pay for their college or make bequests to charitable institutions, think through the implications of what the money or assets will mean to those who receive it and how it can help enrich their lives.

4. Be Charitable

Giving your time and money is an admirable way to live. Giving to those charities, causes and ministries that inspire you is also a great legacy.

Sam's Story:
A Cautionary Tale

One of the reasons we love to share stories of individuals' successes is because they inspire us at Buffini & Company and we hope they inspire you. But I'm about to share a story that's a cautionary tale. It's the only story in the book in which we change the person's name, but all the other facts are true.

"Sam" grew up in Eastern Europe and as a young boy had a real interest in trains. In time, he became a train engineer and was ultimately promoted to the management team that oversaw all the train routes in his country. In the aftermath of a war that tore his country apart, however, he was left without work and made the courageous decision to immigrate to America.

Eventually Sam brought his wife and children to live with him in California. Sam became a house painter (a job close to my heart) and when I hired him to paint my home, he did such a fantastic job that I began to refer him to my friends and business associates.

Sam's business continued to grow. One day we went to lunch and I shared with him the Sequence to Financial Success and the advice I've outlined in this chapter. From time to time I'd check in with Sam and, from what I could see, he was doing great. Sam purchased his first home for $195,000 and within three years it was worth $450,000. His gross income had doubled and he had invested in rental property. And when I asked him whether he was following the Sequence in order, he always said yes.

Then I got a phone call at 3 a.m. the day my family and I were to fly to Ireland on vacation. It was Sam and he was in a complete state of panic. A rare virus called Guillain-Barré syndrome had struck his 19-year-old son. He had symptoms of paralysis and his lungs were shutting down. Of course I empathized as one father to another, but I had no idea why Sam was calling me. Then Sam blurted out, "Brian, I don't know where else to turn. We have no health insurance."

I rushed to the hospital where an administrator told me the treatment might require a six-month hospital stay and cost between $250,000 and $500,000. Sam made too much money to qualify for Medicaid, which would have covered his son's medical costs. I signed a personal guarantee so the hospital would continue his son's treatments.

Because Sam had made *success* investments and bypassed the critical stability piece of the Sequence—which includes being adequately insured—he was in financial trouble. Once Sam got past his son's immediate medical emergency, he agreed that he had to take personal responsibility for his son's medical bills. Sam was forced to sell his rental property and his family's home. The housing market had tanked and Sam sold his properties for 80 cents on the dollar. Sam learned a very hard lesson about the importance of following the Sequence. Here was a man who had done so many things right, and one missed piece undermined everything he had built.

Five years later, Sam has recouped almost all his losses, but it's been a long road back. In sharing the principle of Sequence, I hope you will take a second look at your financial situation. If, like Sam, you've jumped ahead to Success without having all the components of Stability in place, you're out of Sequence.

When you stay in Sequence, you'll quickly discover that the road from financial survival to personal significance is a clearly lit path that, if taken, will allow you to live the good life!

Once you have handled your personal finances, you're ready to delve into the world of business finance. In the next chapter, you'll learn about takin' care of money in your business.

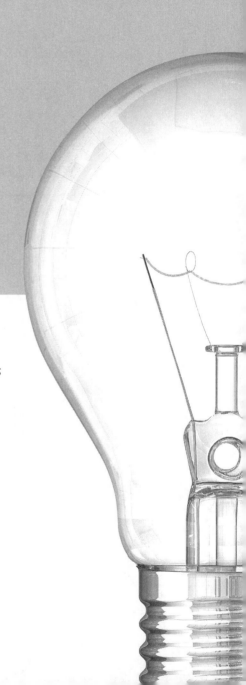

Takin' Care of
Money

Brian Buffini

*My problem lies in reconciling my gross habits
with my net income.*

– Errol Flynn

Takin' Care of Money

Brian Buffini

N o one ever started a business with the intention of not making a profit. Yet most of us put our passion and energy into running our businesses on a day-to-day basis and not on tending to company finances, even though we're usually the Chief Financial Officer in addition to being the CEO. So it's hardly surprising that the third leg of the business stool (Finances) can become cracked and brittle through neglect. And during times when your business is stressed, the financial leg buckles when you most need it to support your company. That's when entrepreneurs find themselves staring at their accounts receivable and payable on their home computers late at night and asking, "How am I ever going to get ahead?" For some small-business owners, it may already be too late.

Lucille Ball got laughs when she asked, "How can I be out of money? I still have checks, Ricky." But real-life money problems can be soul-destroying for a small-business owner. Buffini & Company has coached more than 75,000 small-business owners, and the typical concerns we hear are:

▶ "I don't know where all the money goes."

▶ "I have good months, and I have bad months."

▶ "I can't budget because I don't know what's coming in and when."

▶ "How much money do I take out of the business for myself?"

▶ "How can I get a loan for my business?"

▶ "I don't have time to do anything more than I'm doing."

Paying regular attention to your finances is a must. No small business will prosper if its finances are not in order. Not knowing where your business stands financially is like playing a game of basketball and not knowing the score or the time; it becomes an aimless pursuit. You'll make poor, uninformed decisions. You may choose to expand, purchase equipment or hire staff when your company can't afford it. You're running your business on instinct rather than from a detailed financial map of where you are and where you want to go.

> *Not knowing where your business stands financially is like playing a game of basketball and not knowing the score or the time; it becomes an aimless pursuit.*

One of the great joys Joe and I share is getting a chance to help small-business owners turn their companies around. Typically, we first get them focused on generating new customers—the Big Idea for Small Business. Then we teach them how to take care of their customers by doing The Unexpected Extras, which creates advocates for their businesses. But the most dramatic and immediate turnaround results we see are when small-business owners improve their finances. Here are the steps we recommend to fortify this leg of your business.

1. Budget Your Expenses

"I can't budget because I don't know how much income is coming in," is an all-too-common complaint—and one that is based on a false assumption. You budget *expenses*, not income. Regardless of whether you bring in any income, there are certain fixed expenses you must pay, such as rent, phone and employee salaries.

Step one is to create a working budget. Before you start gritting your teeth at the thought of listing every last expense— "How much *did* I spend on paper clips last year?"—rest assured that I'm not asking you to do that. A working budget starts with a list of your largest fixed expenses, such as rent, payroll, insurance, phone, etc.

Next, make a list of your largest irregular expenses. These are expenses that you might incur once a quarter, biannually or annually. Examples would be property taxes, vehicle registrations, and annual fees or dues. Now make a list of all your miscellaneous expenses, such as copying and printing, stationery, etc.

You've just developed a budget that will make you aware of where your money is going. In the months to come, you can refine it by adding other expenses as you pay them.

Having your finances in black and white in front of you will help you make informed decisions.

What's important now is to review your expenses in detail at least once a month. One of the greatest assets of an entrepreneur is the trust they place in their gut feelings. The downside to this gift is that, without information, they make decisions based on emotions. Having your finances in black and white in front of you will help you make informed decisions. Unfortunately, business owners who review their budgets monthly are decidedly in the minority.

2. Forecast Income

To use an automobile analogy, a budget is your rear-view mirror. It's an analysis of what you've done and where you've been. In contrast, an income forecast is your front windshield. It's what creates the visibility for you to move forward. The most obvious way to forecast your income in the next 12 months is to analyze what you did in the previous 12 months. This is your baseline. Then you adjust for market conditions and changes in your pricing, product offerings or distribution strategy.

The classic mistake most entrepreneurs make is being too optimistic in their income forecasts. A good rule of thumb is to take 20 percent off the top of your best estimate, and most times your forecast will be accurate. If that discourages you, use your adjusted forecast as motivation to beat your number.

In any case, a forecast is simply an estimate of the income you're hoping to produce. At least every quarter and, if possible, every month, analyze your actual performance and readjust your forecast.

3. The Purpose of Business Is to Make a Profit

It's amazing to me how many business owners can't cite how much profit they've made in a given year. Instead, they'll tell you how they *feel* about their businesses. A basketball coach whose team lost by 50 points can say, "I feel really good about my team" and mean it. But there is no erasing the fact that the team still lost by 50 points. For the business owner, *Income - Expenses = Profit.* I'm not suggesting that the only reason to have a business is to make a profit, but without profits, there will be no business to have.

> *Profits are the fuel that keeps the engine of your business going.*

If you aren't personally motivated by money, that's fine. But understand that profits are the fuel that keeps the engine of your business going. And just like the road to hell is paved with good intentions, many well-intentioned businesses have gone to hell by not pursuing profits.

Your business finances must be a priority. Make sure profitability is always part of your decision-making process. Many entrepreneurs who love their work and have a passion for their business ultimately become frustrated and discouraged because the business doesn't yield an economic benefit for them personally. Make sure this doesn't happen to you. Be mindful of your profits or you'll be out of business.

4. Prepare for the Inevitable Lean Times

A mentor of mine once told me, "No one ever went out of business because they had too much cash." When your business is at an all-time high and the economy is surging, that's the time to build up your cash reserves so they can support your company when leaner years arrive. During the recent recession, many businesses foundered because their owners had used their peak income years as the baseline for their future budgets. When business turned down, they found they had invested all their excess capital in an expansion that the market would no longer support.

> *Make sure profitability is always part of your decision-making process.*

Just as you should maintain an emergency fund to cover several months of expenses in your personal life, your company also needs cash reserves. Initially aim to keep cash in reserve to cover one month of your business' expenses and then set a goal to build it up to cover three months of expenses.

You may think that investing your excess capital will provide a better return on your money than leaving it sitting in cash. But even the wealthiest corporations keep cash reserves on hand to keep their operations stable during downturns. Follow Bill Gates' example in running Microsoft®. He endeavored to keep up to a year's worth of expenses in cash, which allowed Microsoft to weather many economic storms. Reserving enough cash to pay one month's worth of business expenses will give you a great sense of confidence and stability.

5. Be Cautious with Debt

Advice on how to get a loan to start or expand a business or to finance inventories is the number-one request of small-business owners, according to the National Federation of Independent Business. Debt can be either beneficial or detrimental to a business. During the start-up phase, it's very common for a business owner to look for investors, partners or loans. This is a very dangerous way to begin your enterprise, however. Based on my experience, there are many more businesses that fail following this path than those that succeed.

Many times, the motivation behind the need for an investment or a loan to capitalize the business is that the business owner is trying to grow his or her business too quickly. Starting a small business has enough challenges without the added pressure of having to validate your decisions to investors—who are perhaps not that sophisticated and may expect a high return on their investment in too short a period of time. Sometimes owners will enthusiastically present the opportunity to investors and create unrealistic expectations that now have to be fulfilled.

If you self-fund your business, it might take five years to reach the same level of growth that you may have achieved in one year with investors behind you. However, after five years, you would own your business 100 percent. You can make decisions that are in your best interest—not the investors'. Oh, by the way, you get to keep the profits!

Business debt has worked well for me in certain cases, such as leasing equipment, obtaining short-term lines of credit and taking out a mortgage on office buildings. But I've ultimately come to the conclusion that the less debt a business has, the better.

6. *Take Chips off the Table*

Every business goes through natural phases of growth, maturity, profitability, decline and, hopefully, reinvention. Each phase does not produce the same level of profitability. To ensure that you aren't depleting your company's assets by paying yourself too high a salary, I recommend that you withdraw a monthly salary that meets your family's basic needs and pay yourself a bonus at year-end from a portion of your company's profits. Some years your bonus will be large; other years there may be no bonus at all.

This disciplined approach has multiple advantages. First, it forces you to keep your lifestyle expenditures under control. Second, when you receive your bonus in a lump sum, you're more likely to do something good with it, like invest it! A word of caution here: don't invest your bonus in your business or in other companies in your industry. Investing your assets in diversified investments reduces volatility and provides the greatest financial security. If your company or industry takes a financial hit, you don't want all your assets to drop in tandem.

And finally, getting a consistent paycheck every month prevents you from spending too lavishly when business is booming or being consumed by worry when business is slow. One strategy that has been profitable for me is to buy the building that houses my business. Being your own tenant and ultimately paying off that building is a great way to take chips off the table and benefit personally from your business.

Mark's Story:
Know Your Numbers to Find Your Niche

Mark Niego, Joe's brother, studied marketing in college. After graduation, he started his own construction business, just like his father. Mark's attention to detail and commitment to excellent service generated more clients than he could handle within a few years.

From the outside, it appeared that Mark's business was a smashing success. But behind the scenes it was a different story. Mark spent nearly all of his time consumed by the demands of the job and gave scant attention to his business finances. He had no budget, and though he tried to keep expenses down, he had no real idea of what he was spending. To keep up with customer demand, Mark reinvested most of his revenue into his business, acquiring office space and heavy equipment and hiring more staff.

After Mark got married and started a family, he realized his take-home income wasn't nearly what it should've been. He reached out to his brother Joe for help. Just like many of the entrepreneurs we've helped through Buffini & Company, Mark was growing his gross income but not paying attention to the bottom line. He knew he had to get a better handle on his finances.

His wife, Cassandra, worked with him to create a business budget, a monthly profit and loss statement, and a cash-flow analysis. By looking at the numbers, Cassandra and Mark realized that some construction projects were far more profitable than others—specifically room additions and kitchen renovations.

In many ways Mark's story is the classic example of the Big Idea for Small Business. Now that he understood the type of clientele he wanted to attract and the niche in the construction industry he wanted to fill, he aligned all his marketing efforts to achieve this. Mark is now very specific when he asks his customers for referrals. He's not just looking for referrals for construction jobs; he's looking for clients who want the type of room additions and kitchen renovations that are profitable for his company. Mark's collateral marketing materials and his monthly mailings are designed to educate his customer base about the niche he now fills in the construction industry.

The *"Mark of Excellence"* is both the slogan for Mark's business *(www.markniego.com)* and a description of his life. After building three strong legs of his business stool, he has a business he loves, customers he enjoys and work that is profitable. He's now able to spend quality time with his family and friends, he volunteers his time and money to help disadvantaged kids, and he coaches youth basketball.

Mark is Working by Referral and living the good life!

There's Nothing Small
About Small
Business

Brian Buffini

*The world was built to develop character. And
we must learn that setbacks which we endure
help us keep marching forward.*

– Henry Ford

There's Nothing Small About Small Business

Brian Buffini

D uring the Roaring '20s Calvin Coolidge famously declared, "The business of America is business." And Coolidge wasn't talking about multinational corporations.

According to the National Chamber of Commerce, almost 90 percent of American employers have fewer than 20 workers. Small business has been, and will always be, the cornerstone of the free-market system. Approximately 50 percent of the U.S. GDP comes from small business and, following a recession, approximately 80 percent of all new hiring comes from small business. Small business is a really big deal, and small businesses don't work without entrepreneurs like you.

What we love about entrepreneurs is their willingness to assume risk. We're willing to bet on ourselves and believe that the market will pay us exactly what we're worth.

> *Small business has been, and will always be, the cornerstone of the free-market system.*

We're willing to work without the safety net of a salary, we believe in our ideas and ourselves, and we trust that if we do enough of the right things, we're going to win. Fortune favors the bold and the brave. And it should. Small-business owners are the straws that stir the drink of every economy.

The Ripple Effect

By its very nature, a small business needs other businesses to support its operations. For example, a contractor will need help from a website designer, suppliers for inventory and tools, an accountant to do his taxes, a printer for his stationery and marketing collateral and so on. The typical small-business owner we coach at Buffini & Company does commerce with up to 20 other businesses per year. Your small business is a pebble in an economic pond, and when you're growing, expanding and hiring, your company has a positive ripple effect on other companies in the community.

So understand that your small business is not *small in significance*. Yes, become successful for yourself and your family. But make no mistake; you're also making a substantial contribution to the local economy and your larger community.

> *Small-business owners are the straws that stir the drink of every economy.*

The U.S. Small Business Administration reported that in the last decade alone, small businesses created nearly 70 percent of all jobs in the United States. The report states, "…where thriving, vibrant small businesses and the entrepreneurs who lead them are in evidence, so too might the heroes of the next economic turnaround be found…" And a Harris Interactive poll found that 66 percent of adults felt that small-business owners are most likely to rescue the economy.

So small businesses don't just offer a livelihood for our families, our employees and ourselves; they are also a vital engine that drives the U.S. economy. The mere existence of small businesses adds to the economic prosperity that we all enjoy.

If at First You Don't Succeed...

Outside the realm of entrepreneurs, many believe that successful people and companies have never put a foot wrong, made a poor decision, had a bad year or faced failure. They imagine that these companies' productivity and income growth trajectory resembles a 45-degree line that shoots up forever.

We know that the truth, however, reads more like a Shakespearean play. Any successful business owner honest enough to relate the unvarnished history of his or her company will talk about the tribulations interspersed between the victories; the highs

> *The mere existence of small businesses adds to the economic prosperity that we all enjoy.*

and lows; and the seasons of stagnation that seemed to drag on indefinitely. They can tell you that success typically follows a pattern of two steps forward and one step back, rather than a meteoric rise to the top. There will always be challenges; what matters is how you respond to them, which can either make or break your company.

Following are a few of our favorite success stories, complete with all the hardships and persistence that created great characters and fortunes.

A Setback Is a Setup for a Comeback

The man behind the ubiquitous JCPenney™ stores—there are now more than 1,100 of them in the U.S. and Puerto Rico—was James Cash Penney, who opened his first store in 1902. By 1912, Penney had 34 stores, 120 stores by 1920, and 1,400 stores by 1929. Then came the stock market crash of 1929 and the subsequent Great Depression, which left Penney in financial ruin. During this period, he had to borrow against the cash value of his life insurance policy to meet the day-to-day expenses of his stores.

These financial setbacks so affected Penney's health that he was admitted to the Battle Creek Sanitarium in Michigan. But Penney persevered, and as he recovered his fortune, he not only discovered a new strength of character, he also became spiritually in tune and financially more philanthropic than ever before. Along the way, he mentored young men such as Sam Walton (founder of Walmart™) and financially supported the lectures and writings of Norman Vincent Peale, author of "The Power of Positive Thinking" and one of the giants of the personal-growth and self-development movement.

Penney's character was formed in the fiery furnace of business adversity, and he emerged not only with a great business and fortune but also as a great man.

Never Give Up on Your Dreams

Actor, writer and director Sylvester Stallone left the University of Miami, where he was studying drama, to pursue an acting career in New York City. By 1973, the 27-year-old Stallone had gone on thousands of acting calls with little to show for his efforts. He was down on his luck and, reportedly, even had to sell his dog to survive.

On March 24, 1975, Stallone watched journeyman boxer Chuck Wepner take on the reigning champion, Muhammad Ali. Wepner knocked Ali down in the first round, only to receive one of the most vicious round-by-round beatings in the history of heavyweight fighting.

But still, Wepner wouldn't go down.

Stallone was inspired by what he had seen and began writing the screenplay for *Rocky*. He presented it to a Hollywood studio that had bought some of his previous work. The studio executives offered to purchase the script with Ryan O'Neal in mind to play the lead. But Stallone's dream wasn't just to make money; his dream was to be an actor. And he saw himself in this role. The studio increased its offer, but Stallone held out for the lead. Stallone got the part—and considerably less money than the initial offer for the screenplay. And the rest is history.

What does Sylvester Stallone's story have to do with you pursuing your business dream? Everything! Behind almost every business success story we know, there were usually multiple struggles for financial survival. But just like Rocky Balboa and the real-life Stallone, if you can take the hits, keep moving forward and embrace that never-say-die spirit, you, too, can be victorious in your business pursuits.

Success at Any Age

Colonel Harland Sanders, the founder of Kentucky Fried Chicken®, had tried many jobs when, at the age of 40, he decided to open his own business. He cooked chicken dishes and other meals at his service station in Corbin, Kentucky, and served customers in his adjacent living quarters because he didn't have a restaurant. As the popularity of his food grew, Sanders built a 142-seat restaurant. When a fire destroyed the restaurant, Sanders rebuilt it along with a motel. Over the next nine years, Sanders perfected his secret recipe for frying chicken in a pressure fryer.

If you can take the hits, keep moving forward and embrace that never-say-die spirit, you, too, can be victorious in your business pursuits.

But when Interstate 75 was completed, motorists no longer had to travel on the north-south route that took them past Sanders' restaurant. Sanders' business soon failed and he went broke. But even though he was 65 years old then, Sanders had a dream of rebuilding his business.

With little more than his $105 monthly Social Security check, Sanders hit the streets to offer his chicken recipe to existing restaurateurs if they would buy his franchise. After more than 100 presentations,

You're never too old or too young to be successful in business.

he finally got one person to agree to his deal. And that was all the encouragement Sanders needed to keep going.

Over the next 10 years, Colonel Sanders sold more than 600 KFC franchises in the U.S. and Canada, and ultimately he sold his business in 1964 to a group of U.S. investors. He also mentored a young man by the name of Dave Thomas, who founded Wendy's® and became a major success story in his own right.

You're never too old or too young to be successful in business. If you are willing to pursue your passion with an unwavering focus, you, too, can be the next Harland Sanders or Dave Thomas.

Make Sure You Have Three Legs to Stand On

The Big Idea for Small Business is that you must put the highest priority on Sales & Marketing in your business; this leg of the stool is five times more important that either of the other two. That doesn't mean, however, that you can forget about the other two legs. Focusing on Customer Service is crucial and attending to Financial Management is essential if you want to own a successful small business.

When all three legs are strong, your business will provide you and your family with economic security and financial freedom. You'll be pursuing work that you are passionate about, and your company may even create employment opportunities for your family members or those in your community. Owning your own business may give you the chance to mentor and develop leadership in others and to engage in philanthropy.

When you apply the Big Idea for Small Business, not only will you be takin' care of business, you'll also be takin' care of your family, your employees and your community. And that's a real big deal!

BRIAN BUFFINI

Brian Buffini was born and raised in Dublin, Ireland. A life-long entrepreneur who has owned many businesses from real estate to retail, he immigrated to America in 1986 and, through trial and error, developed a methodology for generating a consistent stream of high-quality repeat customers.

In 1995, he founded Buffini & Company to share his Working by Referral system with others. Headquartered in Carlsbad, California, Buffini & Company is now recognized as the nation's leading small-business coaching and training company. Bringing years of small-business success and experience to the table, Buffini has provided expert training to more than 2 million people in more than 37 countries.

 www.facebook.com/brianbuffini

 www.twitter.com/brianbuffini

JOE NIEGO

Joe Niego grew up in a blue-collar family on the south side of Chicago. Along the way he has owned a mortgage company and a real estate brokerage; he's also been a pro athlete and a real estate investor. As a youngster, he worked in his family cement business where he learned that the quality of your work is the best possible advertising. Niego attended Lewis University and played basketball alongside his three brothers. Although he majored in marketing, his ultimate dream was to play in the NBA and in 1987 he was the second draft choice of the Houston Rockets.

At the end of his playing career, Niego put the same drive and determination into his real estate career. He excelled in the industry and quickly became one of the top real estate agents in the United States. Three times in his career he sold 30 homes in 30 days! (The average Realtor sells six homes a year!)

In 1994, he opened Niego Real Estate (*www.niegorealestate.com*) and has served more than 2,500 families on the south side of Chicago. Joe has mastered the Working by Referral system not only to build a great real estate career but also to become a great businessman.

He began speaking and training on behalf of Buffini & Company in 2002 and has become one of the most sought-after presenters in the small-business world.

 www.facebook.com/joeniego

ADDITIONAL RESOURCES

To learn more about products and services for individuals
and organizations based on
"Takin' Care of Business: *The BIG IDEA for Small Business"* visit:

www.buffiniandcompany.com
1-800-945-3485

 www.facebook.com/brianbuffini
www.facebook.com/joeniego

 www.twitter.com/brianbuffini

ALSO AVAILABLE

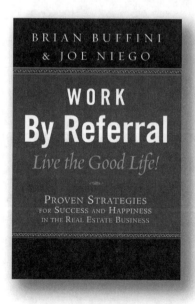

Purchase at:
www.workbyreferralbook.com